Science education
for citizenship

Science education for citizenship

Teaching socio-scientific issues

Mary Ratcliffe and Marcus Grace

Open University Press
Maidenhead · Philadelphia

Open University Press
McGraw-Hill Education
McGraw-Hill House
Shoppenhangers Road
Maidenhead
Berkshire
England
SL6 2QL

email: enquiries@openup.co.uk
world wide web: www.openup.co.uk

and

325 Chestnut Street
Philadelphia, PA 19106, USA

First Published 2003

A catalogue record of this book is available from the British Library

ISBN 0 335 21085 6 (pb)   0 335 21086 4 (hb)

Library of Congress Cataloging-in-Publication Data
CIP data applied for

Typeset by RefineCatch Limited, Bungay, Suffolk

Printed in Great Britain by Bell and Bains Ltd, Glasgow

Contents

Acknowledgements

We are very grateful to all teachers who have participated in the collaborative research described in this book. Pseudonyms are used throughout.

The authors and publisher would like to thank the following for permission to include material originating from them: *New Scientist* for Boxes 6.1 and 6.3; the *Guardian* for Box 1.4; The Association for Science Education (ASE) for Figure 1.1.

If any material is included here which has not been fully acknowledged we would be grateful if we were informed so that we can make the necessary recognition.

Preface

We have written this book based on the view that students should consider socio-scientific issues in the course of their formal education. This should lay the foundations for decisions and actions in adulthood in relation to controversial science-based problems of society.

There are issues in addressing socio-scientific issues in schools related to:

- the multi-faceted nature of socio-scientific issues;
- selection of suitable learning and assessment strategies;
- the pedagogical skill of the teacher;
- the nature of the school curriculum.

We address each of these in this book. In particular we draw on research case studies of innovative practice in relation to socio-scientific issues in order to demonstrate and examine what is possible in 'ordinary' classrooms.

What this book aims to do is to explore the nature of socio-scientific issues and their place in the curriculum; and provide research evidence and guidance for teachers of science, citizenship and humanities in dealing with socio-scientific issues.

We necessarily have to limit our scope. What we do not do is explore all aspects of socio-scientific issues in depth; consider curriculum structures; or evaluate the teaching and learning of underpinning science concepts.

Chapter 1 discusses the multi-faceted nature of socio-scientific issues by exploring the complexities of two topical concerns. Chapter 2 then considers the place of socio-scientific issues in the curriculum by discussion of the purposes of education for citizenship, scientific literacy and sustainable development. In Chapters 3 and 4 we turn to the practicalities of assessment and learning strategies in considering appropriate learning goals and how they may be achieved. Chapter 4 also introduces case studies of innovative learning strategies in action in ordinary classrooms. The case study chapters which follow (Chapters 5–8) describe and evaluate teacher action and pupil learning in relation to ethical reasoning, use of media reports, decision-making strategies and project work. The final chapter discusses the nature of effective teaching and considers a possible future for the teaching of socio-scientific issues.

As science educators we present and discuss examples of assessment, learning and teaching which have been undertaken within science classrooms.

We are of the view that science teaching has much to offer in considering socio-scientific issues. However, we are mindful of the criticisms of science education attempting to embrace all aspects of education for future citizens – literacy, numeracy, social decision-making, as well as introducing students to the major ideas and processes in science. Thus we hope that the issues we discuss are of value to humanities and citizenship teachers, as well as science teachers and educators, interested in social issues with a basis in science.

1 The nature of socio-scientific issues

Which do you prefer – pest-free food or avoidance of long-term damage to the ozone layer? Should vaccination against contagious diseases be compulsory or at patients' discretion? Should research be funded to establish whether there is life in outer space or should priority be given to developing new energy sources?

Of course, the choices are not as stark or as simple as these. The purpose of this chapter is to explore the nature of socio-scientific issues, such as these questions, and possible reasons for their inclusion in the school curriculum. *We consider a socio-scientific issue to be one which has a basis in science and has a potentially large impact on society.*

Interest in socio-scientific issues

Many areas of debate in the media and in social policy relate to socio-scientific issues. As we write this the news headlines are on the radio – they include the Irish government campaigning against a new nuclear reprocessing plant because of radioactive pollution; concerns about the way in which the British foot-and-mouth outbreak had been handled; DNA evidence in a murder trial. These are typical socio-scientific issues which reach national prominence. They can impact on individuals and groups at different levels, from determining policy through to individual decision-making.

Most people are interested in *applications* of science and technology. In 1999, the Office of Science and Technology (OST) and the Wellcome Trust collaborated in research designed to explore attitudes towards science, technology and engineering. As part of the study they surveyed a stratified random location sample of 1839 representative British adults for their interest in particular topics (OST/Wellcome 2000). Almost all were interested in health issues and new medical discoveries (91 per cent and 87 per cent respectively). More people were interested in environmental issues (82 per cent), new inventions and technologies (74 per cent) and new scientific discoveries (71 per cent) than in sport (60 per cent), politics (55 per cent) and economics (48 per cent). Although there are no comparable data for children and adolescents, a declared public interest in science has been shown in previous opinion-poll data of this type (Durant *et al.*, 1989). It is perhaps safe to assume that scientific issues will continue to interest future generations. However, it is notable that in the focus group discussions, as a complementary part of this large-scale research, little interest was expressed in the abstract concepts of science – those largely present in the school science curriculum (OST/Wellcome 2000). Participants were more inclined to discuss the benefits, applications and social use of science and technology. The survey showed that 'interest in a specific area of science is highly correlated with the perceived benefit'. In rating some (given) scientific topics, medical advances and telecommunications which were seen of great benefit were viewed with the most interest. The relationship between science as perceived in the school curriculum – the mastery of some fundamental science concepts – and that of interest and use in adulthood is not a straightforward one. Layton and others (1993) showed that adults use situated scientific knowledge for specific purposes – in which an important aspect is the way scientific concepts are explored in a context specific to the issue under consideration. For example, in dealing with the problems of caring for their Down's syndrome children, parents used their practical knowledge integrated with scientific knowledge they gained from this experience rather than authoritative scientific information given to them formally by experts. Interest and motivation seem high when socio-scientific issues are addressed.

The nature of socio-scientific issues

We will show that socio-scientific issues:

- have a basis in science, frequently that at the frontiers of scientific knowledge;
- involve forming opinions, making choices at personal or societal level;
- are frequently media-reported, with attendant issues of presentation based on the purposes of the communicator;
- deal with incomplete information because of conflicting/incomplete scientific evidence, and inevitably incomplete reporting;
- address local, national and global dimensions with attendant political and societal frameworks;
- involve some cost-benefit analysis in which risk interacts with values;
- may involve consideration of sustainable development;
- involve values and ethical reasoning;

- may require some understanding of probability and risk;
- are frequently topical with a transient life.

Rather than discussing the nature of socio-scientific issues in abstract terms, we will exemplify by considering selected issues – first the use of methyl bromide, an effective and widely used pesticide, and later a bio-medical issue, the use of vaccination for measles, mumps and rubella (MMR).

The use of methyl bromide

Scientific background

Box 1.1   Methyl bromide – background
Methyl bromide has been used for many years as a fumigant for soil before growing crops and in treating harvested crops and warehouses. It boils at a low temperature and easily evaporates. Like many halogenated hydrocarbons, its toxic effects have proved beneficial and problematic. Large-scale use has allowed economic production of a wide range of fruit and vegetables. Methyl bromide does not react with structural materials, is non-flammable and is effective against a wide range of pests. However, like any pesticide its use has to be carefully regulated as it is harmful to the nervous system and major organs such as lungs, liver and kidneys. The major problem with continued use of methyl bromide, however, is that it is a known ozone depletor. As part of the Montreal Protocol its use is being phased out worldwide. There is no simple alternative to methyl bromide, hence its existing extensive widescale use. Research is being undertaken to find the most cost-effective way of controlling pests by alternative methods.

One of the first issues in considering the use of methyl bromide is the nature and presentation of background information. Articles written for an audience seeking technical information abound. The paragraph in Box 1.1 is drawn from a number of sources and tries to present some information about methyl bromide and its use succinctly. There is a high level of technical vocabulary in our summary which assumes some knowledge of science on behalf of the reader. This raises a difficult question. What level of scientific understanding do you need to discuss and develop opinions on a socio-scientific issue? At one level we could argue that a good understanding of, for example, the nature of chemical reaction mechanisms and toxicology is needed to discuss the methyl bromide issue. This is in addition to understanding the nature and generation of scientific evidence. However, many people will develop views on the methyl bromide issue without a detailed understanding of chemical reactions. Interest in the issue, assimilation of information presented in the media and willingness to explore ideas further are features of effective engagement with socio-scientific issues. We consider that we have to assume that key science concepts already part of the school curriculum are an adequate basis for exploration of a socio-scientific issue. The necessary scientific conceptual basis is explored further in Chapter 7. The nature of learning and use of science concepts, such as energy and genetics, is outside the scope of this book. Others have written extensively on the nature and learning of particular science concepts (for example, energy – Solomon 1992a; most concepts in the second-ary curriculum – Driver *et al.*, 1994). There is one area, however, where the current curriculum lacks emphasis and less is known about effective teaching and learning, and that is the nature of scientific endeavour itself. We address learning about the nature of science in several places throughout this book.

Evaluation of information

At this point you may be wondering if you are in for a lengthy and dry treatise on pesticide use. If you thought you were you might stop reading unless you were deliberately searching for particular information. Most of the information we (and school students) receive about socio-scientific issues comes from media reporting – newspapers, TV, radio, Internet. In these media, dense presentation of information would deter all but the most dedicated information seeker. Journalists use particular presentation styles and hooks, such as human drama, controversy, compelling research findings or shock-horror tactics to gain inter-est. How and where information is presented can influence its interpretation.

We have examined a variety of sources in trying to present concisely what is known about methyl bromide. We are conscious as we write this that what-ever we present here, and what the average citizen reads, is inevitably incomplete and selective. Yet we all have to use incomplete information every day in forming opinions and making decisions about our future actions. The information reaching us is presented and filtered in different ways. Farmers who use methyl bromide; atmospheric chemists; environmental activists; government agencies; newspaper journalists may all present the methyl brom-ide issue with different emphases even though they may claim to be unbiased. (Bias is present in what we write here – we are influenced by what we read, our scientific training and our beliefs and values.) How, then, do we decide what information can be trusted? A simple answer might be to rely on the expertise of scientists in evaluating the evidence. However, the public's trust in such expertise is by no means absolute. According to a national study (OST/ Wellcome, 2000), people tend to trust sources seen as neutral and independent – university scientists, scientists working for research charities or health campaigning groups, and television news and documentaries. The least trusted sources are politicians and newspapers, with sources seen as having vested interests (e.g. environmental groups, well-known scientists and popular scientific press) ranking in between. This distrust of newspapers has implications for how reports are interpreted.

Policy makers and the general public may expect scientists to present them with the 'right answer'. After all, this is the view of science they may have developed from their experience at school – exposure to a well-established body of knowledge which helps explain the world and can be built upon in further 'discoveries'. What has been implicit (and far less visible) in much school science up to now is the means by which science knowledge claims are established – an issue of importance in many socio-scientific issues. As soon as we start considering the banning or continued use of methyl bromide, the complexity of the issue is apparent (Box 1.2). One feature of this issue, then, is the nature and limits of the scientific evidence – how certain can we be that methyl bromide is a more efficient ozone depletor than many other halogenated chemicals? How certain are the detrimental effects of ozone layer thinning? What is the nature of the scientific evidence? How was it established? What explanatory theories are being drawn upon? And, importantly, how does this interact with our prior beliefs?

Box 1.2   Methyl bromide – an ozone depletor

The reason for banning methyl bromide as a pesticide is not its inherent toxicity but the effects of its reaction with ozone. Over 100 countries, who signed the 1992 Montreal Protocol, undertook to protect the ozone layer by phasing out production and use of identified ozone depletors. Methyl bromide is considered to be a more effective ozone depletor than many CFCs whose production has already ceased. The evidence for this is based on known reactions of methyl bromide and modelling of the chemistry of the upper atmosphere. There is no easy way of knowing the extent to which methyl bromide *is* responsible for thinning the ozone layer. Ozone layer depletion increases UV-B radiation reaching the earth's surface, which can result in skin cancer and suppression of the immune system.

Local, national and global dimensions

In the case of methyl bromide, the signatories to the Montreal Protocol have erred on the side of caution – banning the use of ozone depletors regardless of other consequences. In any risk-benefit analysis, the implication is that ozone layer protection is a top priority. You may or may not agree with the countries who have signed the Montreal Protocol – certainly environmental pressure groups are keen to see a rapid worldwide ban of methyl bromide whereas farmers may be more reluctant. We could see the methyl bromide debate as a public policy issue. But does the use of methyl bromide have any significance for us at a personal level? This depends on our priorities, values, beliefs and role in society. Even if we are not conscious of the details of pesticide use, our actions as consumers may impact on the issue. In developed countries we take for granted a plentiful supply of pest-free foods. The increase in 'organic' products on supermarket shelves may be a consumer response to a desire for decreased dependence on chemically intensive farming. However, some consumers may consider that organic products are intrinsically nutritionally better. The Parliamentary Office of Science and Technology (POST) report on media handling of the genetically modified (GM) food debate highlights the issues surrounding the import and trials of GM crops, and the ensuing political and media debates as to the safety of GM foods (Durant and Lindsey 2000). This report suggests that concerns over GM foods made a major contribution to the increase in popularity of organic foods. Socio-scientific issues often have local, national and global dimensions, as shown in Box 1.3. These dimensions also relate to the political and societal context within which the issue is being considered – for example the regulatory frameworks that apply and how these relate to local, national and global governments.

Box 1.3   Methyl bromide – local, national, global

Although many countries are phasing out production and use of methyl bromide, they are doing so at different rates. The US is the world's largest user of methyl bromide. The US, like EU countries including the UK, ceased production of methyl bromide in 2001 and will phase out its use by 2005. Some European countries, notably the Netherlands, and the Nordic countries banned use of methyl bromide by 1998. Less developed countries, who were signatories to the Montreal Protocol, aim to phase out use by 2015. Thus the issue has local, national and global dimensions. Different nations and people react to the problem of methyl bromide in different ways. For example, Australia warns its citizens about the dangers of UV-B radiation but has not supported an early phase-out date for methyl bromide – according to an issue of Global Response Action produced by Pesticide Action Network and Friends of the Earth. Farmers in the US who are having to seek alternatives to methyl bromide may resent this international difference given a global market for crops. Food Link News (2000) highlights a particular UK concern. The cereal processing industry relies on methyl bromide to eradicate pest infestations in flour mills. There is no single viable alternative. The problem is particularly acute in the UK because the current Food Safety Act has zero tolerance for insect infestation. The UK has to provide a more stringent insect control programme than that in much of the rest of Europe and the US. These examples illustrate some of the interaction between a global issue and national implementation.

Media reporting

Most people will gain information about socio-scientific issues through national and local media – newspapers, television, radio, Internet etc. The way science is portrayed by these media and interpreted by the receiver has an important impact. In the OST/Wellcome (2000) study 64 per cent of participants agreed with the statement 'the media sensationalizes science'. Journalists may have a number of reasons for reporting socio-scientific issues – one may be to inform but, equally, the purpose may be to provoke reactions. Nelkin argues:

> By their selection of a newsworthy event (e.g. a new AIDS therapy), journalists define pressing issues. By their focus on controversial problems (e.g. the location of toxic dumps), they stimulate demands for accountability, forcing policymakers to justify themselves to a larger public. By their use of imagery, they help to create the judgemental biases that underlie public policy. The media can influence public policy even in areas where there is broad indifference on the part of the electorate.
>
> (Nelkin 1995: 73)

Contrast the information we have presented so far with extracts taken from a lengthy discussion in the *Guardian* newspaper of accumulation of pesticide residues (Blythman 2001) (Box 1.4). This article typifies media reporting of socio-scientific issues. It is based on examination of technical or research reports and tries to acquaint the reader with scientific details in an engaging way. Yet, inevitably, it uses emotive language. This article extends the discussion of methyl bromide to more general issues of pesticide use in food production. There are three aspects, common to many socio-scientific issues, which the article raises:

- evaluation of evidence presented;
- consideration of risk and probability;
- environmental sustainability.

Evaluation of evidence

The article in Box 1.4 is fairly typical in trying to present scientific research in an interesting way. Statistics are scattered throughout ('72% of the apples we ate contained residues' 'a lettuce is typically treated with 11.7 pesticide applications') without detail of the way in which the data were collected and interpreted. This is not sniping at journalists – they are restricted in the space available, the editing done and their interpretation of data. Yet, such use of

Box 1.4   Extracts from a newspaper article about pesticide residues in food

Toxic shock   *Guardian*   **Saturday 20 October 2001**

With a third of all the food we eat containing them, pesticide residues have become a routine ingredient in our diet. Something needs to change. But with a hit-and-miss monitoring programme, current farming practices and a complacent government, is that likely, asks Joanna Blythman.

Every autumn, the government publishes a complex and daunting document reporting on pesticide residues in the food we eat. Although the detail varies from year to year, the underlying picture is the same. Buried among all the opaque, technical language and optimistic, bureaucratic spin, a persistent reader will always find the annual shockers. These are the foods that have clocked up residues over 'toxicologically acceptable limits', such as carrots with 'unexpectedly high' traces of acutely toxic organophosphates or pears with enough illegal growth regulator to cause 'a mild stomach upset in toddlers'. Then you come to the bulk of findings that simply reflect the extent to which pesticide residues have become a routine ingredient in our diet. Last year, 67% of the grapes, 72% of the apples and 71% of the pears we ate contained residues . . .

Some 86% of consumers polled last year told NOP that they did not want any residues in their food. Their concerns might be eased if the government was seen to be on the case. Comfortingly, the government's Pesticide Safety Directorate (PSD) assures us that it is 'committed to ensuring the safety of food' and that, accordingly, it carries out 'a comprehensive monitoring programme for the presence of pesticide residues in food on sale in the UK'. The truth is rather different. The UK has one of the weakest residue-testing regimes in Europe. New pesticides are constantly approved via a system designed to provide a market for the agrochemical industry, rather than to defend public health, and any progress towards removing old ones that do not meet even the current questionable safety requirements is alarmingly slow. In fact, the problem is getting worse . . .

While there are serious questions about the validity of the government's figures, it would be wrong to suggest that the PSD is supine when these figures highlight a problem. One such problem is lettuce, especially the commonly eaten 'flat', or butterhead, lettuce. It is more prone to intercepting and retaining pesticide residues than, say, an iceberg, because of its open, leafy shape. Lettuces have been sampled almost every year since 1994 because tests have revealed high levels of several pesticides, including two illegal ones, chlorothalonil and vinclozolin, both so-called 'gender-bending' or endocrine-disrupting chemicals with proven anti-maleness effects. Over the years, warnings have been issued to growers and legal action taken. But why are flat lettuces so bad for residues? As well as being open and leafy, they are grown all year round in a 'protected environment' under glass or polytunnels, unlike icebergs, which are largely grown outdoors (but not in winter due to the risk of frost). The protected environment creates the perfect climate for the growth of pests and diseases, so chemical treatments are required . . .

General housekeeping out of the way, you come to the vexed question of soil sterilisation. There's no point in trying to grow protected lettuces in a conventional system without it. The standard kit for the job used to be methyl bromide, rated by the UN as a 'Class One' ozone depletor. Now that it looks as if it may be banned by 2005 due to international pressure, growers must start looking for more benign alternatives . . .

It therefore comes as no great surprise to find that a lettuce is typically treated with 11.7 pesticide applications throughout its growing season. Nor is it hard to see why the UK happens to have a little running problem with residues in this salad crop. One can appreciate, too, that if a grower is locked into this type of production, it must be tempting to slosh on a little bit of extra illegal this or that. But, equally, one cannot help but be awed by what is demanded of growers. It is clearly no longer enough to be a good gardener; you need a degree in chemistry and plant biology, too . . .

There is no doubt that an obsession with the cosmetic look of fruit and vegetables has led to an overuse of pesticides. These 'beauty pageant' standards are enshrined in the EU's fruit and vegetable grading scheme, which reserves the grades 'Extra Class' and 'Class 1' – the classes supermarkets seek – for strictly catwalk produce. To qualify for membership of these classes, it isn't enough just to look good; the produce has to be of uniform shape and size, too. The consequences of this obsession have been devastating. The main reason that 71% of the pears we ate last year had residues, for example, is that the trees had been treated with chlormequat, a pesticide growth regulator used for cosmetic purposes to 'improve' the shape of the fruit . . .

Yet unless the government adopts an unequivocal pesticides reduction policy, residues in food will continue to creep up, leaving concerned consumers with several options. You can switch to organic. You can try to minimise residues by scrubbing and scraping your food to within an inch of its life, though that will remove only some of the surface residues, not those that lie deep in the flesh. You could ditch healthy eating entirely and live on a diet of heavily processed, nutritionally depleted food so as to limit your exposure. Or you could just accept that every third mouthful of food you eat contains poison. Are you up for that?

quantitative data can raise more questions than answers. The nature of scientific research presented in media reports is discussed further in Chapter 3.

Risk and probability

The final paragraph of the article (Box 1.4) presents the reader with three choices concerning pesticide residues. What are your reactions? How do we

weigh the risks and benefits of banning methyl bromide (a social policy decision)? How do we weigh the risk of accumulation of pesticide residues in our
food against, say, consumption of high-cholesterol foods or 'beef-on-the-
bone' (individual action)?

Simon Jenkins, a newspaper columnist and critic, implies that risk analysis
is a straightforward business in his quote related to the likelihood of contracting nvCJD from BSE-infected beef:

> I want to know, from those more knowledgeable than I, where a steak
> stands alongside an oyster, a North Sea mackerel, a boiled egg and
> running for the bus. Is it a chance in a million of catching CJD or a
> chance in 10 million? I am grown up; I can take it on the chin.
>
> (Durant 1996: 14)

Even if scientists could indicate with certainty the probability of developing a
particular disease from the intake of known amounts of toxic compounds,
would that in itself change people's dietary habits? Understanding of probability helps put risk and opportunity in perspective but it is the interaction
with our values and prejudices which determines any action we might take.
No activity is risk-free. Millions buy lottery tickets in the hope of winning large
sums of money, yet the same people might avoid eating a particular food
because it carries a similar, very low, probability of harm. We are not rational in
our actions. We tend to accept voluntary risks, such as driving a car and smoking, far more readily than involuntary risks, such as environmental hazards
related to new planning proposals. However, 'educationally and culturally to
understand the concept of "risk" is crucial', as Crick argues in his consideration of the relations between science and citizenship, particularly in considering media communications (Crick 2001: 33).

Sustainable development

In developed countries we take plentiful supplies of food for granted – as the
article in Box 1.4 appears to do. Use of fertilizers, pesticides, growth-regulators
– whether manufactured or organic – is inevitable in large-scale food production to fulfil the world's needs. There is a complex relationship between consumers, producers and supermarkets. Is the demand for a particular food (e.g.
imported fruit such as mangoes, kiwi fruit) generated by the supermarket promoting the product or by consumers seeking it? Whatever the reasons, we end
up in developed countries having a vast choice of fresh and processed foods.
The global implications of this are complex – does production of coffee in
Columbia for export help improve the lifestyle of Columbians? If we are going
to consider food production and pesticide use in any depth we encounter the
issue of sustainable development.

Ask people 'on the street' about the meaning of the term sustainable development, and you will find that very few know or have a ready answer, and virtually all the responses will be different. This is hardly surprising since sustainable development is a complex, multi-faceted concept, which combines aspects of environmental protection with social equity and the quality of human life. Indeed, there are over 65 definitions of the term in circulation (Symons 1997), but two of the most commonly quoted are:

> Sustainable development [means] improving the quality of human life while living within the carrying capacity of supporting ecosystems.
>
> (UNEP/WWF 1991)

> Sustainable development is development that meets the needs of the present without compromising the ability of future generations to meet their own needs.
>
> (WCED, 1987)

Sustainable development is therefore essentially characterized by the simultaneous struggle for environmental protection and economic development. The more developed countries have long experienced an uneasy relationship between these two goals, and it was only in the 1980s that society began to accept the notion that lack of development (i.e. poverty) can damage the environment as much as development.

We need to address three fundamental concepts in order to achieve sustainable development, each with underlying and often overlooked complexities:

- The concept of development. This is not the same as economic growth, which is effectively quantitative expansion. Development is a qualitative concept which includes economic aspects, but also cultural and social elements such as 'improvement' and 'progress' which are often more subjective and less easily measured.
- The concept of needs. This is a relative term; the needs of the rich are luxuries to the poor. Realistically, for poor countries to meet their needs rapidly, the burden on the environment would be intolerable under the current economic systems.
- The concept of future generations. We cannot predict what scientific knowledge, skills or resources will be available to future generations, or what resources our descendants will value. Of course, they in turn will not be able to predict the needs of subsequent generations, and so the safest, but most difficult, solution at present is to find ways of ensuring the sustainable and equitable utilization of all resources

(including potential genetic resources). These solutions will inevitably have to come from a combination of scientific and social endeavours.

All three concepts include a strong element of citizenship. They underline the importance of making decisions based on the best possible scientific information, and increasing people's awareness of the part that their personal choices can play in delivering sustainable development.

Ethics and values

So far we have exemplified, with methyl bromide, that socio-scientific issues:

- have a basis in science, frequently that at the frontiers of scientific knowledge;
- involve forming opinions, making choices at personal or societal level;
- are frequently media-reported, with attendant issues of presentation based on the purposes of the communicator;
- deal with incomplete information because of conflicting/incomplete scientific evidence, inevitably incomplete reporting;
- address local, national and global dimensions, with attendant political and societal frameworks;
- may require some understanding of probability and risk;
- involve some cost-benefit analysis in which risk interacts with values;
- may involve consideration of sustainable development.

The use of vaccination for MMR

We now turn to a different socio-scientific issue to highlight other important dimensions present – those of ethics and values. We choose to discuss the issue of MMR (measles/mumps/rubella) vaccination for at least two reasons – there has been considerable media reporting on the issue and there are identifiable links with the science curriculum.

Most science textbooks for students up to the age of 16 explain transmission of viral diseases, the body's natural defence mechanisms and use of immunization in artificial production of antibodies. Many texts consider the prevention of disease from a social point of view with advice to prevent the spread of infectious diseases. Few science textbooks debate the wider personal and social impact of the disease or vaccination. The science teacher is encouraged to help students understand the nature of disease transmission and its prevention but may be discouraged from considering the social impact. In contrast, the social impact of disease transmission may be a dominant feature of humanities' curricula – the history of medicine allowing opportunity to explore changes in medical practice from a social point of view. Students gain understanding in science lessons about the defence mechanisms of the human body, and in humanities lessons about the social issues of disease transmission. The compartmentalization of the secondary curriculum often prevents the two perspectives from being considered together. Surely the social and scientific perspectives together are important in being able to consider socio-scientific issues effectively. This dichotomy is slowly changing with the introduction of the citizenship curriculum and recognition of the status of 'scientific enquiry' within the science curriculum. Science Year projects (ASE 2002) and the work of the Pupil Researcher Initiative (PRI 2001) are just two examples of production of curriculum materials which attempt to encourage discussion of issues such as immunization.

The vaccination case study of the Pupil Researcher Initiative project (PRI 2001) presents some simplified articles about the issues surrounding the use of MMR vaccine, in particular the evidence for and against the links between vaccination and autism and issues of relative risk. Students are encouraged to distinguish 'fact' from 'opinion' and consider relative risk. Some of the questions they are expected to answer include those in Box 1.5, which address issues of probability and risk.

Box 1.5   Some of the questions posed for students in considering media influences on safety of vaccines (PRI, 2001)

Before you start . . .

You are vaccinated to protect against diseases that used to harm or kill people. Imagine one of the vaccines carries a tiny risk that you may lose your hearing. What level of risk are you prepared to accept?

1 in a 100   1 in 10,000   1 in a million   None at all

After the activities . . .

Q1 A newspaper article can change people's point of view about a scientific issue.

       (a)   How did article 2 try to persuade you that the MMR vaccine is risky?

       (b)   What effects can newspaper 'scare stories' have on the public?

Q3 The chances of a measles vaccine having a serious side effect are 1 in a million.

      How safe do you think the vaccine is? Explain your choice.

      Not safe?   Quite safe?   Very safe?

The immunization case study on the ASE Science Year CD ROM – 'Can we; should we?' (ASE 2002) presents a variety of perspectives. Like the PRI materials, one activity is based on distinguishing fact from opinion. Another focuses on evaluating arguments and a third (Figure 1.1) explores the concept of a 'free rider', the person who benefits from the contributions of others without themselves making any contribution. The teachers' notes accompanying this activity clarify the difference between a 'free rider' and someone who makes their decision by evaluating relative risk. This approach starts to engage the student in considering risk and values.

It is interesting to note in passing that both these sets of materials imply, but do not openly state, that their authors support MMR vaccination and the scientific evidence in its favour. The stance of the teacher (or that embedded in curriculum materials) is a crucial issue when bringing socio-scientific issues into the classroom. Should we adopt a role of neutral chair regardless of strength of evidence on each side of an issue, play devil's advocate or declare our own views? These issues are considered in Chapters 4 and 7.

Embedded in both of these examples of curriculum materials, besides probability and risk, are consideration of ethics and values. In previous work on the ethical aspects of science, definitions of science and ethics have been given (Fullick and Ratcliffe 1996: 7) as:

> Science – the process of rational enquiry which seeks to propose explanations for observations of natural phenomena.
> Ethics – the process of rational enquiry by which we decide on issues of right (good) and wrong (bad) as applied to people and their actions.

In identifying these as processes of rational enquiry, scientific conduct and ethical conduct are both based on norms of systematic procedures, even-handedness and openness. Science has its own ethical principles, crucial for the proper conduct of science. These principles include intellectual honesty, open-mindedness, accuracy in data collection and reporting, suspension of judgement, a self-critical attitude. Although scientists aspire to sound ethical conduct, we have to recognize that we are fallible beings with individual values and beliefs, particularly when we consider the outcomes of science in society. Our values stem from a complex mixture of belief systems and cultural norms. Our beliefs, both religious and otherwise, are based on upbringing, education and social influences. These are mediated by cultural 'norms' of home, school and wider society. The importance or value an individual places on a particular facet of an issue may depend upon these cultural norms. For example, although some values such as honesty, compassion and mutual trust are universally prized, appearance and aesthetics may have higher esteem in some communities than wealth and economic value and vice versa.

What if everyone did that?

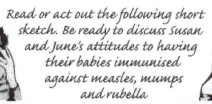

Read or act out the following short sketch. Be ready to discuss Susan and June's attitudes to having their babies immunised against measles, mumps and rubella

Susan and June, both young mothers with babies, are sitting in the park watching their older children play

June: We're taking little April for her MMR jab tomorrow, I hope she'll be alright.

Susan: You're mad! Why are you even risking it?

June: We'd rather run the risk of her having a bad reaction to the jab than getting one of those diseases.

Susan: But those old diseases have virtually disappeared now, there's virtually no chance of her getting one of them.

June: But the diseases have disappeared *because* people get their children immunised.

Susan: Yes, but they *have* disappeared, so now there's no need to worry.

June: But if people don't get their babies immunised the diseases will come back.

Susan: Yes, but that's *people*, not *you*. There'll always be plenty of goody-goodies who do what the doctors say, so why should you risk April's health when you've no need to?

June: Well, we're not risking it very much, the doctor told us that the chances of her being badly affected or affected at all, given our family history, are very low indeed.

Susan: Yes, but why take any risk at all? As long as other people are having their babies done, why take the chance? I'm certainly not going to risk my Danny.

Susan thinks that it's stupid to immunise your baby (and so run the small risk of the baby being badly affected by the vaccine) so long as enough other people are getting their babies immunised to make it unlikely that your baby will get the disease.

1 Is Susan right?
2 If you don't think Susan is right, how might you get Susan to change her mind?

Figure 1.1 The idea of a 'free-rider': curriculum materials

Wellington (1986) highlights how a consideration of values is one facet of a 'controversial' issue. His definition of a controversial issue indicates how the nature of the issue itself provides a motivation for discussion.

> A controversial issue must
> - involve value judgements so that the issue cannot be settled by facts, evidence or experiment alone;
> - be considered important by an appreciable number of people.
>
> (Wellington 1986: 149)

In a similar vein, the Crick Report defines a controversial issue as 'an issue about which there is no one fixed or universally held point of view. Such issues are those which commonly divide society and for which significant groups offer conflicting explanations and solutions' (Advisory Group on Citizenship 1998: 56).

This societal division of views brings personal morality and public morality into contrast. A major element in our own value judgements is personal morality – what we regard as instrinsically right or wrong (as opposed to the ethics of *how* we make decisions). In making moral judgements we can express our own views, but we also have to be conscious of the social context of the issue. For example, if we believe that the MMR vaccination is morally right not just for our child but for all children, do we have the right to impose this on others (an issue of public morality)? Warnock (2001) shows that public morality is enshrined in legislation which seeks to promote shared values acceptable to the vast majority. She argues that legislators must be seen to be informed, rational, consistent and mindful of long-term consequences. Warnock chaired the Government Committee of Enquiry into Human Fertilization and Embryology, the legal outcome of which was that it is permissible, subject to the licensing of each research project by a statutory body (the Human Fertility and Embryology Authority), to use a human embryo for research for up to 14 days from fertilization in the laboratory, and then to destroy it. Warnock highlights differences between private and public morality:

> . . . there is a difference between what is a generally agreed moral view (as, for instance, that children should not be used as subjects of research) and a morality which, though not agreed, is nevertheless broadly *acceptable*. When I first came across the use of the word 'acceptable' in this kind of context, I thought of it as a typical civil service cop-out. It was, I thought, mealy-mouthed. They, the civil servants, did not want to use strong and definite words which would commit them, words like 'right' and 'wrong'. But I came to see that I was here confusing private with public morality. In public issues

where there is a radical difference of moral opinion (as between those who think the early embryo should have the same moral status as a child and those who do not), and where no compromise is possible, the concept of the acceptable is a useful and indeed indispensable one.

(Warnock 2001: 70)

This notion of *acceptability* in public morality is one we consider important when discussing socio-scientific issues with students. As Warnock (2001: 156) argues, 'to think in ethical terms *is* to think generally, searching always for agreement, or possible agreement, in the values involved'.

Controversy, values and scientific evidence

We consider that controversy about contemporary science and its uses can arise in two main ways.

Type A The social application of well-established science, for example vaccination or management of toxic chemicals.

In cases like these, the main issues for discussion are to do with the interaction of other dimensions, such as ethics, politics, economics, with the existing scientific evidence – that is, issues are discussed and opinions formed in terms of competing values, impact on people etc.

Some teachers may thus consider that discussion of socio-scientific issues is not the business of science lessons. Others may consider the applications of science as of prime importance in helping students put their experience of school science in context. Research evidence (for example Solomon 1993) suggests that students are interested in socio-scientific issues and these have the potential to put the science in context and increase motivation.

In many cases, analysis of the issue is by examining risks and benefits, weighing up alternatives, considering different factors and points of view. The focus is not mainly on the nature of the scientific evidence but on its implications.

Type B Societal discussion of the implications of 'science-in-the-making', for example the nature of 'global warming' or ozone layer destruction.

In cases like these, the issues discussed in Type A apply but, in addition, there is controversy over the nature of the scientific evidence. To engage in effective consideration of such cases, people need to have some understanding of the ways in which scientific evidence is generated and used.

The distinction between Type A and Type B is not clear-cut. There are limits to existing scientific evidence. Thus, understanding the nature and generation of scientific evidence is important. The processes and practices of science are implicit in most science classrooms. Students develop an awareness of the nature of science through the activities in which they are engaged. Unfortunately, these experiences can sometimes reinforce some common myths about the nature of science. In order to be able to deal with scientific controversy, it helps to make the processes and practices of science more explicit. McComas and colleagues (1998: 6) recognize that 'at the level of fine detail there will always be active debate regarding the ultimate level of science'. However, from examining science education documents around the world, they propose that there is a consensus about the view of science which can be presented to students (Box 1.6). Recent empirical research of what experts consider should be taught *about* science supports most of this consensus and adds further detail (Osborne *et al.*, 2001). We may find that students believe one or more of the common myths about science (Table 1.1), because of the way scientific endeavour is presented. Just as ideas about electricity, photosynthesis etc. need clear explanations to aid understanding, the main ideas and terminology of the nature of science need highlighting and explaining.

Box 1.6   A consensus view of the nature of science objectives extracted from eight international science standards documents (McComas *et al.*, 1998: p 6)

- Scientific knowledge while durable, has a tentative character
- Scientific knowledge relies heavily, but not entirely, on observation, experimental evidence, rational arguments and scepticism
- There is no one way to do science (therefore, there is no universal step-by-step scientific method)
- Science is an attempt to explain natural phenomena
- Laws and theories serve different roles in science, therefore students should note that theories do not become laws even with additional evidence
- People from all cultures contribute to science
- New knowledge must be reported clearly and openly
- Scientists require accurate record keeping, peer review and replicability
- Observations are theory-laden
- Scientists are creative
- The history of science reveals both an evolutionary and revolutionary character
- Science is part of social and cultural traditions
- Science and technology impact on each other
- Scientific ideas are affected by their social and historical milieu

Table 1.1   Common myths about the nature of science (after McComas, 1998)

Myth	Correction
Hypotheses become theories which in turn become laws	Laws are generalizations or patterns Theories are explanations of those generalizations
Scientific laws and other such ideas are absolute	Scientific laws have limitations and can be subject to revision
A hypothesis is an educated guess	Hypothesis could mean (i) a 'generalizing' hypothesis (which might become a law); (ii) an 'explanatory' hypothesis (which might become a theory); (iii) a prediction
A general and universal scientific method exists	No research method is applied universally. Scientists approach and solve problems with imagination, creativity, prior knowledge and perseverance
Evidence accumulated carefully will result in sure knowledge	It is impossible to make all possible observations and to secure facts for all time
Science and its methods provide absolute proof	Accumulated evidence can provide support for a law or theory but never prove them to be true
Science is procedural more than creative	It is the creativity of individual scientists which allows them to go beyond the evidence and develop laws and theories
Science and its methods can answer all questions	Science cannot answer moral, ethical, social, aesthetic questions
Scientists are particularly objective	Scientists are no different in their objectivity than other professionals. They do try to be careful in analysis of evidence
Experiments are the principal route to scientific knowledge	Scientific knowledge is gained in many ways including observation, analysis, speculation, library investigation and experimentation
Scientific conclusions are reviewed for accuracy	The number of findings from one laboratory checked by others is small
Acceptance of new scientific knowledge is straightforward	If an idea is a significant breakthrough or change, its acceptance is by no means quick or easy
Scientific models represent reality	Scientific models are created to describe aspects of the natural world and are useful in giving predictions and explanations
Science and technology are identical	Pure science is the pursuit of knowledge for its own sake. Technology, or applied science, is exploitation of science
Science is a solitary pursuit	Scientists work in teams

In considering the nature of socio-scientific issues, the final dimension we wish to raise is that of topicality. The examples we have shown here are ones which seemed relevant at the time of writing. We have no way of knowing whether these same issues seem pertinent or important as you read this. This starts to raise the main issue of this book. How do we prepare students to consider socio-scientific issues of the future when we can only guess at the nature of scientific advancements and social dilemmas? In the next chapter we start to grapple with the aims of education to deal with socio-scientific issues. We discuss views of 'citizenship' and 'scientific literacy' in locating the purposes of this book.

2 Socio-scientific issues and the curriculum

In attempting to define notions of citizenship, scientific literacy, environmental education and sustainable development, there is a great temptation to search for links and areas of overlap among them. However, this can be an unrewarding endeavour since they all have different meanings and purposes in the minds of different people. These concepts defy succinct, crisp definitions that are capable of revealing their true meaning in a few words. This is because the ideas are far-reaching and all-embracing in nature, and depend on criteria used to judge supporting concepts such as democracy, or the quality of life. It could be argued that such definitions are actually unnecessary, and it is sufficient to say that we intuitively appreciate the need for these concepts without having to define them, in the same way that we appreciate the need to condemn crime or eliminate poverty and disease. It is our view that, in the context of education in schools, all these concepts at least play a part in, and some possibly even map perfectly onto, the overarching notion of citizenship. They all contribute towards providing students with the knowledge and skills to play an effective role in society, through being informed, thoughtful, caring and aware of their rights and responsibilities.

Even if there is difficulty in articulating concepts relating to science and citizenship education, we feel it important to discuss such meanings in locating socio-scientific issues in the curriculum. Thus the following sections explore the nature of the terminology and concepts used: education for citizenship; scientific literacy; sustainable development.

Citizenship

Citizenship is a contested and slippery concept. Kerr (1999) suggests that differing views about the function and organization of society are at the heart of the contest. Two main styles of citizenship, reflecting this point, can be identified – a civic republican tradition, derived from Ancient Greek society, which stresses duties; and a liberal tradition, dominant during the last two hundred years, which stresses rights. Heater (1999: 165) uses these styles and other principles to suggest that there are a number of different types of education for citizenship depending on the underlying principles and focus. A purpose of citizenship education from a civic republican perspective is to produce partici-pant and patriotic citizens, whereas a liberal style promotes support for democracy. Other principles such as moulding for particular socio-political purposes can result in the production of 'robotic' citizens or training of elite citizens. If a geographical level is the underlying principle, the purpose of education for citizenship can be to promote identity at different levels from national through to global with a hope of combating xenophobia, war and environmental degradation. This last principle has some resonance with pur-poses of environmental education (see pages 29–34) and is taken up by Oxfam in promoting a functional perspective that a global citizen:

- is aware of the wider world and has a sense of his or her own role as a world citizen;
- respects and values diversity;
- has an understanding of how the world works economically, politic-ally, socially, culturally, technologically and environmentally;
- is outraged by social injustice;
- participates in and contributes to the community at a range of levels from the local to the global;
- is willing to act to make the world a more equitable and sustainable place;
- takes responsibility for his or her actions.

(Oxfam, 1997: 2)

Whatever perspective on citizenship is adopted:

Citizens need knowledge and understanding of the social, legal and political system(s) in which they live and operate. They need skills and aptitudes to make use of that knowledge and understanding. And they need to be endowed with values and dispositions to put their knowledge and skills to beneficial use.

(Heater 1999: 164)

This recognition of knowledge, skills and values is promoted in the attainment expected of students following the citizenship curriculum in England where the knowledge base is of the rights, responsibilities and duties of citizens; the role of the voluntary sector; forms of government; and the criminal and civic justice, legal and economic systems. Skills of using and evaluating information, including the media, and participating in school and community-based activities are put alongside expectations of opinion forming and personal and group responsibility (DfEE/QCA 1999: 31). However, as Heater points out, 'beneficial' use of knowledge and skills is subjective depending on the political and societal context – hence his categorization of citizenship education according to some political ideals. In the English National Curriculum, with an emphasis on responsibility with accompanying rights, it is not entirely clear who determines what constitutes responsible action. Perhaps an appropriate summary is one of the learning goals that Lynch (1992: 43) identifies – 'autonomous but socially responsible moral judgement and integrity, based on reflective and clarified values'. As Lynch indicates, such a goal can only be achieved by students participating fully in their own education. Citizenship education is not a passive pursuit by students. It involves clarifying values, evaluating information and viewpoints, discussion, decision-making and action.

Kerr contends (1999: 9) that we lack understanding of many areas of citizenship education in practice. For example, among other things, little is known about:

- the strategies, resources and approaches employed by teachers in the classroom;
- the outcome of citizenship education programmes;
- the extent and type of knowledge and understanding 11- to 16-year-olds have of society;
- the relationship between knowledge, attitudes and behaviour among this age group;
- the degree to which schools, teachers and the curriculum can affect the acquisition of social knowledge by students and influence their attitudes and behaviour.

We cannot embark on citizenship education without considering the values inherent in the issues considered or the personal and societal perspectives brought to bear. Layton (1986) identifies three stances on values education:

- inculcation – certain values are instilled by repeated exemplification and reinforcement;
- moral development – students are helped to develop more complex moral reasoning patterns often by the use of moral dilemma episodes, with structured small group discussion;
- clarification – students are helped to become aware of and to identify their own values and those of others.

Which of these three dominates depends on the age of the students, the curriculum context and teacher disposition. In the context of socio-scientific issues, particularly in secondary education and beyond, we favour moral development and values clarification related to a framework of social and cultural norms of moral behaviour. However, Marsden (2001) considers that past efforts in education *for* citizenship in the UK and in the US, whether explicit or implicit, have involved inculcation and indoctrination in 'good' behaviour – whether that be related to expected norms of religion or state. Materials from earlier citizenship or civics programmes show the lack of liberal, humanistic goals, sending particular messages about moral and responsible behaviour. This may continue with present UK citizenship initiatives. The current citizenship education programme in England derived from an Advisory Group whose remit was 'to provide advice on effective education for citizenship in schools – to include the nature and practices of participation in democracy; the duties, responsibilities and rights of individuals as citizens; and the value to individuals and society of community activity' (Advisory Group on Citzenship 1998: 4). Thus the expected outcomes of citizenship education reflect this starting point of participation, responsibility and community action. Marsden (2001) wonders whether citizenship education exemplifies what Findlay (1920) warned of as the 'naïve faith in schooling as a grand panacea for human ills'. It would be easy to see science education for citizenship as placing on future generations the skills and responsibilities to solve previous generations' environmental and science-related problems. However, throughout this book we try to take a realistic stance on the nature and potential of 'science education for citizenship'.

Scientific literacy

'Science literacy, or as many people say, scientific literacy, is vital to participation in modern society. However, that is about the end of the agreement as scientific literacy is a fuzzy concept that masks many different meanings' (Savelsbergh *et al.* 2001: 2).

We will not debate all the meanings and nuances of scientific literacy here (for fuller accounts see, for example, Shamos 1995; Levinson and Thomas 1997). Rather we seek to identify main issues in considering the links between scientific literacy and citizenship.

In providing one overview of the concept of scientific literacy, Laugksch (2000) identifies different factors that can influence interpretations of scientific literacy: the nature of the concept of scientific literacy and how it is defined in different contexts; the possible purposes of scientific literacy and how these can be measured; the interest groups with views on conceptualizing and implementing scientific literacy. He presents these factors in a diagram to which we have added a summary of components he discusses under each factor (Figure 2.1). This diagram serves to summarize some of the

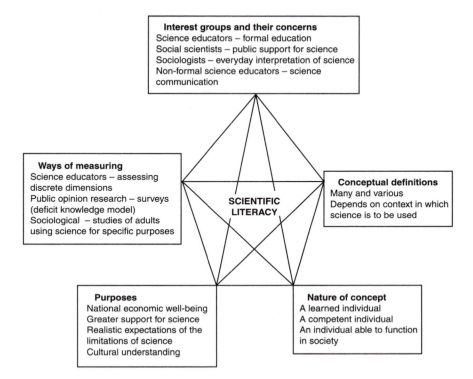

Figure 2.1 Factors that influence interpretations of scientific literacy: A conceptual overview (adapted from Laugksch 2000: 74)

conflicts that appear when scientific literacy is discussed. There are several groups with expertise and a legitimate interest in defining 'scientific literacy'. We concentrate on formal education but we note the different purposes and ways of measuring 'scientific literacy' – from discrete scientific knowledge in supporting economic well-being to use of science for specific purposes in promoting realistic expectations of science. Should the aims of formal education focus on developing the wealth of the nation through a workforce with a good understanding of science concepts or on personal understanding of the cultural achievements of science? Should we value achievement shown through mastery of discrete knowledge and skills or that shown by holistic interpretation of real issues? These are dilemmas to which there may be strong individual views but no ready answers. However, we consider formal education concentrates currently on the former at the expense of the latter in each case.

There is little research on the interaction between formal education and the use of science outside school by children and adolescents. A deficit view of the public understanding of science is that the problem with the general public (and, by extension, adolescents) is that they lack the background understanding of scientific concepts and all that is needed is additional information. Adopting a stance of science education as providing just knowledge and understanding of science concepts has significant limitations. Studies of adults show that adults can access detailed and complex science knowledge for their own purposes when they have a particular problem or question – often related to their lifestyle (Layton *et al.* 1993; Irwin and Wynne 1996). Engagement with science can be seen as evaluating expertise; deciding which information sources to trust; considering risks and benefits. Indeed Layton *et al.* (1993) found that 'practical science knowledge in action' had to fulfil the criteria of being: of obvious relevance; helpful and useful; from a trustworthy source; relatable to other social knowledge; and in accessible communication rather than the formal language of science. Formal education, besides providing a background in science concepts, ought to provide students with skills with which to explore scientific issues presented in the future. As Jenkins (1997) argues, for most citizens interest in science and technology is linked to decision-making and action. The notion of 'functional' scientific literacy (the third possible nature of the concept in Figure 2.1) is perhaps closest to this perspective of how adults can behave. We consider that it is only through engagement with all aspects of socio-scientific issues that students can develop understanding and skills to assist their future decision-making and actions.

Just as there are debates about the nature and purposes of scientific literacy, there are also different views on appropriate curriculum content. We are drawn to Law *et al.*'s (2000: 147) analysis of how the alternative perspectives can determine the balance of content for scientific literacy (Figure 2.2). People who regard the science disciplines as important to the well-being of society value traditional, academic science content. Others have a focus on the individual general citizen, privileging science as a human activity with its practical reasoning and habits of mind (personal well-being). Others take a more functional and societal perspective (societal well-being), emphasizing a small number of key scientific ideas, their societal, cultural and technological development and impact. The societal and personal well-being priorities, combined with attitudes and beliefs (Figure 2.2), have some overlap with citizenship education.

The aspirations of scientific literacy are not without their critics. Shamos (1995) argues that social or civic literacy (citizenship by another name) is really the underlying goal of the scientific literacy and science–technology–society (STS) movement in particular:

> It is time we all recognize this as an impossible task and get on with the normal business of science education. Not even professional

Figure 2.2 The scientific expert approach to defining the content of a school science curriculum for scientific literacy (Law *et al.* 2000: 147)

scientists can always be relied on to vote with their heads instead of their feet, and no *reasonable* amount of science education can ever get the average person to the point where he or she is able to judge such issues independently and dispassionately.

(Shamos 1995: 216)

We totally agree with his analysis of human behaviour. Indeed, in recognizing that values, attitudes and scientific knowledge are intertwined in making judgements, we consider that this interaction should be explored explicitly in formal education rather than ignoring or comparmentalizing the components. Shamos's answer to developing social literacy is to 'emphasize the *proper* use of scientific experts, as an emerging field that has not yet penetrated the science curriculum'. He recognizes that this may not be easy, but argues for an educational approach in which students recognize and value scientific experts, particularly in determining social policy. This is in sharp contrast to views expressed by two Australian science educators (Cross and Price 1999). They argue that relying on experts is a disturbing trend with 'the rise of expertocracy with its accompanying interests, both political and economic, being identified as a threat to democracy'. Perhaps what both these perspectives imply is that students should begin to recognize the nature of scientific expertise, the reasons why experts disagree, and the problems which occur when this happens, and the way in which scientific expertise is portrayed in the media – all issues which we consider contribute to science education for citizenship. However, none of these curriculum commentators presents evidence of what might realistically be achievable in terms of specific learning and teaching goals in 'normal' classrooms.

Despite his antipathy to scientific literacy, in his curriculum guide for 'scientific awareness' Shamos emphasizes the nature of scientific and, importantly, technological endeavour. Besides features of the nature and development of science and technology, Shamos argues for the inclusion of: the societal impact of science and technology; the role of statistics; the role of risk-benefit analysis in decision-making; the proper use of expert science advice. We do not see this as dissimilar to calls for evolutionary change in the science curriculum to fulfil goals of scientific literacy, with an increased emphasis on technology and ideas-about-science (nature, processes and practices) as well as key explanatory stories providing a holistic overview of the great ideas of science (Millar and Osborne 1998). This outcome of *Beyond 2000*, a Nuffield Seminar Series, argues that among the aims of the science curriculum should be that students can:

- appreciate why the important ideas and explanatory frameworks of science are valued;
- appreciate the underlying rationale for decisions (for example about diet, or medical treatment or energy use) which they may wish, or be advised, to take in everyday contexts, both now and in later life;
- understand, and respond critically to, media reports of issues with a science component;
- feel empowered to hold and express a personal point of view on issues with a science component which enter the arena of public debate, and perhaps to become actively involved in some of these;
- acquire further knowledge when required, either for interest or for vocational purposes.

(Millar and Osborne, 1998: 2012)

The *Beyond 2000* report has proved influential in shaping some of the directions of the English science curriculum.

The overlap between scientific literacy and citizenship

In considering the connection between scientific literacy and citizenship, at least two distinct and well-established areas of endeavour can be identified – STS education (science–technology–society) and environmental education. In highlighting these stances, which have much in common, we note that lack of interchange of literature and ideas is a feature even in these closely related areas.

STS education

It could be argued that 'science education for citizenship' is STS education by another name. Both have an emphasis on personal and societal decision-making. As Solomon claims (1994: 192), 'the highest aims of STS education relate to how our students will behave as citizens'. (However, see Chapter 3 for difficulties in evaluating this fine educational goal.)

The nature and history of STS education in the UK and internationally is explored in many publications (see for example, Solomon 1993; Solomon and Aikenhead 1994; Ratcliffe 2001). Essentially a product of the 1970s and 1980s, in most countries STS education has not become a central feature of science, technology or, where it exists explicitly, citizenship education. Technology has perhaps been the most neglected and underrated aspect of STS education.

In 1994 Layton wondered if STS education was being overtaken by events:

> If we were to have a science curriculum in education with a focus on authentic science and an understanding of science in its social contexts, and if we were to add to that a separate technology curriculum that emphasized problem solving and inventions in the practical world, then what would be the role of STS? Insofar as the science and technology curricula need supplementation, it would probably come from the field of practical ethics and moral education. Was STS a coalition of its times and is now in need of reformation?
>
> (Layton 1994: 42)

We leave you to judge to what extent this comment on science and technology curricula is true in your context. What is apparent is the decline in the use of the term STS in more recent educational publications, particularly in the UK.

Environmental education

People's perception of environmental education varies considerably. Many still regard environmental education initiatives as tending to focus on a limited number of well-documented environmental disasters, or individual campaigns, often fronted by non-governmental organizations such as Greenpeace or the Worldwide Fund for Nature (WWF). However, researchers and specialist teachers in this field generally agree that environmental education should encompass economic, social and cultural issues and their relation to the environment – thus the recent tendency to refer to environmental education as *education for sustainable development.*

So what content and teaching approaches should environmental education programmes include if they are to engender an environmental ethic among students? And how does this overlap with science and citizenship education? Fien (1993a) discusses three main recognizable approaches, or biases, in teaching environmental education (EE):

1   The 'knowledge approach' (education *about* the environment) is the most common form of environmental education in schools. The aims are to emphasize knowledge about natural systems and processes (for example the hydrological cycle, food webs, and the mechanisms of climate change and ozone depletion) and the ecological, economic and political factors that influence decisions about how people use the environment. This approach is often represented in existing science and geography courses.
2   The 'needs of society approach' (education *through* the environment) is a learner-centred approach, using students' direct experiences of the environment as the medium for education. It aims to add reality, relevance and practical experience to learning by immersing students in the values conflict over a local environmental issue, such as recycling schemes, transport systems, or green consumerism.
3   The 'critical enquiry approach' (education *for* the environment) builds on education about and through the environment to develop a sensitive environmental ethic, through a critical examination of values and attitudes, and alternative solutions to environmental issues. It involves developing informed concern for the environment, a sense of responsibility, active participation in resolving problems, and the communication and participation skills that are needed if we are to guarantee environmental protection.

The first two approaches are, unsurprisingly, much commoner in schools, with constraints on time and the curriculum, but theorists generally agree that 'education for the environment' – a critical enquiry approach – is essential in order to develop lifestyles compatible with the sustainable and equitable use of resources. This third approach thus parallels aims of citizenship education.

Although researchers and policy makers do not always agree about the specific content or teaching methods in environmental education, certain general features are commonly advocated in the academic and professional literature. One view that prevails among specialists in this field is that the most effective approach to environmental education in schools is one which is holistic in nature, being integrated across the whole school curriculum (for example WCED 1987; Palmer and Neal 1994; Tilbury 1995). As a consequence, environmental educational resources and study packs for schools have steadily moved away from their origins in the scientific paradigm, towards a broader range of value-centred methodologies (Palmer 1998). These encourage students, teachers and local community organizations to work together on socially critical investigations, where there is overt commitment to social justice and responsibility. With this inclination towards linking environmental, economic and social issues, it follows therefore that there is an increasing acceptance among researchers that environmental education teaching should centre around the principles of sustainable development (for example Fien 1993a; Sterling 1996). Tilbury (1995) promotes this as the focus for environmental education, and identifies a number of key characteristic components. These include a holistic approach, work which is relevant to the learner, a strong values education component, issues-based learning, an action-oriented approach, development of socially critical skills and a futures perspective (Box 2.1). This approach could be valuable for any socio-scientific issue and is very similar to approaches advocated by STS educators.

Political literacy has also been cited as a key feature of any effective environmental education programme (for example Huckle 1985; Tilbury 1995; Sterling 1996) in that it is necessary to resolve real environmental and development issues. Palmer (1998) and Fien (1993b) also stress the importance of recognizing the variety of stances, ideologies or 'worldviews' on the environment. Even people who consider themselves to be 'environmentalists' are likely to have a variety of stances over issues such as animal rights, technological solutions to environmental problems, or the extent to which their own personal quality of life should be compromised for the sake of environmental protection. Fien usefully places these different worldviews on a continuum of 'environmental politics', ranging from 'technocentrics' to 'ecocentrics'. A 'technocentric' worldview regards people as separate from nature and sees nature as a resource to be conserved in the interest of people; an 'ecocentric' worldview reflects a view that people are part of nature, that nature should be conserved for its own sake, and that nature provides a metaphor for morality and a guide to the way we should live. Recognition of these perspectives helps people begin to articulate their own views and make sense of the diverse views held by others, which they are likely to encounter in the debate surrounding sustainable development issues.

Despite the difficulty in defining the term, there is a growing consensus among governments, industry and the public that we need to move urgently

---

Box 2.1 Components of environmental education for sustainability (after Tilbury 1995)

Relevance – to the contemporary lives of the learners (life at work and at home, etc.), and to the needs of society

Holism – addressing environmental problems holistically; including scientific, aesthetic, economic, political, cultural, social and historical dimensions, and higher level thinking skills.

Values education – beliefs, attitudes and convictions that determine one's decisions and behaviour. Involves accepting values of others, sense of responsibility, harmony with nature and stewardship. Development of a *personal environmental ethic* involving elements of equality, equity and sustainability.

Issues-based learning – identifying and investigating issues, seeking solutions, carrying out actions to address issues, evaluating the impact of environmental actions.

An action-orientated approach (active learning strategies) – encouraging participation through: negotiation, persuasion, consumerism (for example boycotting, 'green' choices), political action (through the democratic process), legal action, ecomanagement.

Critical enquiry – including critical reflective knowledge, critical thinking skills, democratic skills and values, and experience of the process of environmental politics. This helps develop *politically literate individuals*. Socially critical skills are vital to understand the complexities of sustainability. At the root of critical thinking are questions such as:

Who makes decisions affecting environmental quality?

Why are they made?

According to what criteria?

Are long-term consequences considered? What are they?

A futures perspective – probable futures and possible alternative futures.

How can we move towards a sustainable future locally, nationally, globally?

---

towards more sustainable lifestyles if future generations are to enjoy quality of life. Instrumental in ensuring that education for sustainable development (ESD) gained a firm place in the statutory science curriculum was the Sustainable Development Education Panel, which was set up by the UK government to make practical recommendations for action on ESD in schools, further and higher education, at work, during recreation, and at home.

Box 2.2   Seven concepts of sustainable development

Sustainable Development Education Panel's seven key concepts of sustainable development, and suggested specific learning outcomes for students at the end of primary/beginning of secondary school (i.e. among 11- to 12-year-olds) (from DETR 1999: 37–8):

Pupils should:

1 *Interdependence – of society, economy and the natural environment, from local to global*

Understand how people, animals and plants are interconnected through natural cycles and ecological/biological systems;

Understand that human and natural changes in the environment can harm or enhance the ability of different groups of plants, animals and humans to survive and flourish;

Appreciate the differences or similarities between probable and preferable long-term changes to the environment and society.

2 *Citizenship and stewardship – rights and responsibilities, participation and cooperation*

Want to learn more about their local and global environment and know how they can care for it and improve it;

Be able to work with other members of the school community and feel responsible for improving its sustainability;

Be able to explain how the values and expectations of the school affects their behaviour and how their lifestyles at school and at home depend upon and impact on the environment and other people.

3 *Needs and rights of future generations*

Appreciate that they have choices in the way that they use products and services and that different choices can affect others and the environment differently;

Have begun to be able to distinguish between actions and products which are wasteful or more sustainable;

Understand that some natural resources are finite while others can be used sustainably.

4 *Diversity – cultural, social, economic and biological*

Understand what is meant by biodiversity in local and global contexts and the importance of maintaining biodiversity at local and global levels;

Understand and value 'local distinctiveness' in relation to townscape/landscape, economic life and culture, and habitats;

Know how monitoring the distribution and diversity of species in a habitat can serve as indicators of quality of and change in the environment.

5 *Quality of life, equity and justice*

Know and understand that basic needs are universal;

Understand the reasons why there are differences in the extent to which people's basic needs are met, and that these inequalities exist within and between societies.

6 *Sustainable change – development and carrying capacity*

Have begun to understand the concepts of carrying capacity and limits through, for example, studying overgrazing or road capacity;

Be able to understand how human systems work in terms of simple systems concepts as inputs, outputs, sources, sinks and flows, and consider how they may be managed more sustainably, for example, the house, the school, and the farm;

Understand and be able to develop indicators for their own lifestyle and community that they can use to monitor sustainability.

7. *Uncertainty, and precaution in action*

Understand that people have different views on sustainability issues and these may often be in conflict;

Be able to listen carefully to arguments and weigh evidence carefully.

The panel proposed seven 'key concepts of sustainable development', suggested specific learning outcomes associated with these concepts for children at different ages (Box 2.2), and offered the following definition of ESD in the context of schools:

> Education for sustainable development enables people to develop the knowledge, values and skills to participate in decisions about the way we do things individually and collectively, both locally and globally, that will improve the quality of life now without damaging the planet for the future.

(DETR 1999: 30)

The learning outcomes shown in Box 2.2 have resonance with the aims of education for citizenship and scientific literacy.

Location of socio-scientific issues in the curriculum

Education for citizenship, scientific literacy and sustainable development all focus on values, conceptual understanding and skills (procedural understanding). The key concepts differ across the three:

Citizenship – rights and responsibilities; legal and political frameworks
Scientific literacy – nature of science; key scientific concepts such as energy, cells, particles
Sustainable development – the nature of sustainability; natural systems and processes.

However, attention to procedural understanding of reasoning and decision-making combined with acknowledgement and elaboration of values is a feature of all three. Socio-scientific issues could feature under any of the three headings: citizenship; scientific literacy; sustainable development. Given this situation we now consider the location of socio-scientific issues within the curriculum.

We have implied that 'science education for citizenship' is principally the province of science teachers. However, the situation is not as simple as that. Dawson (2000) sounds a cautionary note. We agree with his analysis that 'we science educators must recognise the limitations of scientific method and understanding and not try to centre science at the core of all decision-making' (Dawson 2000: 131). We agree that consideration of socio-scientific issues involves many facets, of which knowledge of science content perhaps plays a relatively minor role. Dawson argues that science teachers are not the best people to teach about society and social issues, given their particular educational background. Rather they should concentrate on the features of scientific endeavour and the strengths and limitations of science. 'The development of understanding of ethics, economics and logical argument needs to be tackled elsewhere' (Dawson 2000: 131). While we have considerable sympathy with this view, the subject structure of the curriculum could result in two extremes:

- Students consider socio-scientific issues in lessons other than science, developing skills of reasoning, communication and analysis, yet not necessarily appreciating the strengths and limitations of scientific processes and content in addressing the issue. In this scenario, science lessons can be seen as devoid of social context and unrelated to topical issues.
- Students consider socio-scientific issues in science lessons, developing skills of reasoning, communication and analysis, *and* appreciating the strengths and limitations of scientific processes and content in

addressing the issue. However, in this scenario the demands on the science teacher and the science curriculum become all-embracing.

To what extent are socio-scientific issues the province of science education or humanities education? Huckle (2001: 158) describes how geography and English departments in secondary schools cooperated in engaging with the genetically modified food (GM) debate through students' use and evaluation of information on relevant websites. Lessons were intended to explore the 'ways in which language and images communicate risk, uncertainty and trust, and how politicians seek to manage risk in order to maintain public support'. We find it concerning but understandable that science departments were not involved in this cross-curricular initiative. We have heard anecdotally of many instances where the potential for discussion of socio-scientific issues has not been exploited in science classrooms.

Several authors have discussed how recommended practices in environmental education compare with the teaching realities in schools (for example Oulton and Scott 1994; Tomlins and Froud 1994; Robertson and Krugly-Smolska 1997; Grace and Sharp 2000a). Palmer (1998) emphasizes the contradictions that exist between the advocated focus on real environmental issues, which requires a flexible inter-disciplinary approach, and the discipline-based curriculum, which emphasizes abstract theoretical problems. Yet cross-curricular cooperation is lacking in many secondary schools (Oulton and Scott 1994).

Other constraints imposed on the delivery of environmental education in schools inevitably widen the gap between aspirations and practice. A national survey of 294 secondary schools in England and Wales by Tomlins and Froud (1994) identified the main constraints as being lack of time, lack of appropriate resources, lack of appropriate training for teachers, lack of expertise or motivation among some teachers, and the cross-curricular and non-statutory nature of environmental education. Gayford (1991) studied secondary teachers' attitudes and identified constraints in terms of concerns they had with both cognitive and affective aspects of environmental education. This related to staff expertise and included difficulties communicating the all-embracing concept of the environment, the complexity of environmental issues, and the confusing mixture of teaching methodologies and assessment techniques. A qualitative study of teachers in Ontario by Robertson and Krugly-Smolska (1997) also revealed that some teachers felt that they did not have permission to cover controversial environmental issues in ways that theorists propose.

While certain aspects of the rhetoric–reality gap are inevitably created by constraints beyond the control of the teachers, it does not necessarily follow that schools would wish to deliver environmental education as advocated by theorists if these constraints were removed. Accepting the existence of an environmental education rhetoric–reality gap, Grace and Sharp (2000a) explored the nature and size of the gap that might exist if teachers had a completely free choice of content and approaches. Their study sought the views of secondary school teachers with an 'environmental remit' on the importance of 36 components (including content and approaches) of environmental education as advocated by theorists, and found that removal of constraining factors might be expected to have the following effects:

- Five components would be included more readily: *cross-curricular work, use of external experts, involvement with local community initiatives, involvement with local industry*, and *considering the work of environmental and green groups*. These did not form part of the EE curriculum in most schools, but were endorsed by most of the teachers.
- Five components would tend to remain absent: *active learning strategies, parental involvement, involvement with other secondary schools, involvement with other primary schools*, and *older students working with younger ones*. None of these received a positive attitude among the teachers.

This challenges the common assumption that the rhetoric–reality gap would simply close if constraining factors were removed; it seems more likely that the gap would narrow in some respects and widen in others.

We note with concern that active learning strategies would not necessarily increase if constraints to environmental education were removed. We suggest there are a number of reasons for the lack of citizenship in science, most of which relate to the expectations of science (and other) teachers as reflected in their education:

- teachers' lack of confidence or ability in handling issues with no 'correct' answers;
- lack of knowledge/proficiency concerning teaching strategies to cope with controversial issues;
- dealing with large amounts of information, which is inevitably incomplete;
- perceived dominance within the curriculum of acquiring knowledge and understanding concepts – therefore no time for consideration of social and ethical issues;
- perception amongst some teachers that social issues should not be part of the science curriculum;
- logistic (and philosophical?) barriers in cross-curricular collaboration.

It is notable that the first three issues deal with teaching strategies which are familiar to humanities teachers yet can seem alien to many science teachers.

We propose methods to address these issues at a number of points in this book. We return to the place of socio-scientific issues in the curriculum in Chapter 9, after exploring assessment, learning and teaching.

Summary

Socio-scientific issues can feature in education for scientific literacy, citizenship and sustainable development. 'Scientific literacy', 'citizenship' and 'sustainable development' are broad concepts whose wholescale adoption in education has immediate practical problems and far-reaching consequences. An overarching educational aim may be that *students will act as informed, responsible citizens when confronted with future scientific advancements*. This is not a modest goal! However, we suggest that strands of conceptual and procedural knowledge, attitudes and beliefs embedded in the discussion of citizenship, scientific literacy and sustainable development can be the basis for appropriate learning goals. These may go some way towards the elusive and overarching aim. Faced with controversy about the concepts and their implementation and frequently lack of evidence from real teaching and learning contexts we argue for modest goals as achievable ends in such a complex area.

As in socio-scientific issues themselves, the strands of conceptual and procedural knowledge, attitudes and beliefs are not discrete but interrelated. However, emphasis can be given to one dimension over others in particular learning activities. In the next chapter we explore how assessment evidence, mainly from studies without targeted teaching, can inform the elaboration of specific learning goals.

3 Learning and assessment

In the first two chapters we highlighted the nature of socio-scientific issues and their place in science and citizenship education. Our aim in this chapter is to consider how we can identify and evaluate learning goals in relation to socio-scientific issues.

Identifying learning goals

We have already identified key features embedded in consideration of socio-scientific issues. They:

- have a basis in science, frequently that at the frontiers of scientific knowledge;
- involve forming opinions, making choices at personal or societal level;
- are frequently media-reported, with attendant issues of presentation based on the purposes of the communicator;
- deal with incomplete information because of conflicting/incomplete scientific evidence, inevitably incomplete reporting;
- address local, national and global dimensions with attendant political and societal frameworks;
- involve some cost-benefit analysis in which risk interacts with values;
- may involve consideration of sustainable development;
- involve values and ethical reasoning;
- may require some understanding of probability and risk;
- are frequently topical with a transient life.

We can take an atomistic or holistic approach to learning and assessment. At an atomistic level, we can turn each of these features of socio-scientific issues into learning goals in their own right.

We could identify that we want learners to be able to:

- demonstrate understanding of science concepts and the processes involved in scientific research and dissemination;
- recognize and demonstrate understanding of the nature of decision-making at a personal and societal level;
- recognize and demonstrate understanding of the nature, strengths and limitations of media reporting of scientific issues;
- recognize and deal with incomplete information, evaluate evidence;
- recognize the scope of the socio-scientific issue in terms of local, national and/or global dimensions; recognize the political and societal context;
- undertake cost-benefit analysis, recognizing possible different value positions involved;
- demonstrate understanding of the nature of environmental sustainability;
- undertake ethical reasoning;
- demonstrate understanding of the nature of probability and risk;
- recognize the topicality and changing nature of socio-scientific issues.

Another way of considering these learning goals is to recognize the different types of knowledge, understanding and skills. We can re-present these learning goals in a different form:

Conceptual knowledge

Learners can demonstrate understanding of:

- underpinning science concepts and the nature of scientific endeavour (how scientists develop ideas/theories/models; links with systematic data collection; reporting of findings; peer review);
- probability and risk;
- the scope of the issue – personal, local, national, global; political and societal context;
- environmental sustainability.

Procedural knowledge

Learners can engage successfully in:

- processes of opinion forming/decision-making using a partial and possibly biased information base;
- cost-benefit analysis;

- evidence evaluation, including media reporting;
- ethical reasoning.

Attitudes and beliefs

Learners can:

- clarify personal and societal values and ideas of responsibility;
- recognize how values and beliefs are brought to bear, alongside other factors, in considering socio-scientific issues.

Each of these learning goals could be dealt with discretely – an atomistic approach to learning and evaluation, or the interrelated nature of them could be recognized in learning strategies and assessment – a holistic approach. Both approaches have advantages and disadvantages. An atomistic approach could result in good 'performance' in each of these areas but a limited ability to deal with the overall complexity of socio-scientific issues. A holistic approach recognizes the complexity of socio-scientific issues but runs the risk that some appropriate learning goals are not emphasized nor the particular skills and understanding taught.

Evaluation of learning

It is at this point that considering how we can evaluate learning may assist in determining what is *desirable* and what is *possible*. If our main educational goal is to develop students' abilities to take responsible, informed actions when faced with real socio-scientific issues, evaluation of the development of these abilities should take an authentic and valid form – examining students' *actions* when confronted with real issues. There are at least two reasons why such authentic evaluation is difficult to achieve. One is concerned with the relationship between education and behavioural outcomes. Another consideration is the practicality of authentic assessment.

Relationship between opinion, attitudes and behaviour

We will take the intractable one first – is it realistic to expect engagement with socio-scientific issues to change behaviour and to be able to measure this change? For example, through discussion students may come to the view that recycling of domestic waste is an important way to reduce dependency on raw materials. Yet, they may not put this opinion into practice with any regularity. Knowing that smoking, overeating and indulging in too much alcohol are disadvantageous to health does not necessarily stop us. The aims of health education programmes are often to influence behaviour as well as opinions, yet changing established routines is notoriously difficult to achieve.

Lawson (2001) illustrates the difference between opinions and actions and the limited impact of formal education from a citizenship lesson she observed on child labour in India:

Teacher: What can we as consumers do to improve the situation?

Pupil: We shouldn't buy the footballs but the reality is that we won't stop buying footballs or stop playing football. I know it's selfish. It's as bad on the streets as it is in the factory.

Teacher: So are you saying that a certain amount of child exploitation is inevitable?

Pupil: Yes.

Teacher: How many of you realized that Nike trainers were made in these conditions? One or two say they did.

Teacher: How many of you will buy Nike trainers now you know the conditions they are made in?

Nearly all the pupils put their hands up.

(Lawson, 2001: 172)

While influencing actions may be a goal of 'science education for citizenship', it might be more realistic to expect development of opinion and attitude – precursors to action – than changes in behaviour. In addition, evaluating behaviour, particularly in real rather than contrived situations, is fraught with difficulties. Apart from the value judgements involved in assessing actions relating to real problems, there are limitations in the school context of assessing real behaviour with respect to controversial issues. Students' actions with respect to real issues tend to take place outside the classroom in 'everyday' life. The best we can do, perhaps, in formal education is to evaluate opinions and decisions developed in the learning context. This can take the form of exploring students' own opinions or of examining their judgement of others' actions. This is where we return to the discussion in Chapter 1 in relation to ethics and values. An individual viewpoint on a socio-scientific issue may reflect a personal moral perspective, but a public judgement may show what is acceptable through consensus. Two students may have totally different and vehemently held views on, for example, the use of animals in medical research. Is it appropriate for us to judge one student's view as 'better' than the other? We think not. However, what is up for examination is the student's reasoning in reaching this view. Are students able to marshal clear arguments? Are students able to consider and evaluate evidence? Do students consider others' views or dismiss them out of hand? These skills can be addressed through focused learning activities in which formative and peer assessment can aid development. Examples of assessment items discussed below consider this approach.

The practicalities of authentic assessment

There are practical problems in evaluating students' attitudes, opinions and reasoning. We have indicated the multi-faceted nature of socio-scientific issues and the variety of possible learning goals. The practicalities of assessment tend to encourage evaluation (and teaching) of understanding and skills which are easy to assess. Some of the learning goals we suggest are more challenging to assess (and teach) than those relating to recall and simple understanding – currently common in assessment systems.

If we were serious about developing authentic and valid measures of student achievement and progress, we would value multiple forms of assessment – in much the same way as we value variety in learning strategies and recognize the multi-faceted nature of dealing with socio-scientific issues. We would allow students to show their achievements when they felt ready and able, in a variety of forms including student-generated projects and oral assessment. We would value transferable skills and feel confident in making judgements of student achievement based on a portfolio of evidence. As a general rule, the more authentic the assessment, that is the closer to the context within which the skills and understanding are to be used, the greater the validity of the assessment procedure. For example, if we want to evaluate student capabilities of operating as a team member, we need to see how students work with others on different occasions. Equally, if we value 'team membership' as an educational goal we should expect to teach it explicitly, that is help students to understand the features of team membership and develop their individual and collective skills in this direction. Authentic assessment is high in validity but can be time-consuming and requires considerable skill on the part of assessors to ensure comparability of judgement across different contexts and different assessors. Clear, specific criteria for assessment help judgements to become reliable.

Evaluation of learning can be formative or summative depending on the use made of the assessment. Normally we would expect in-class evaluation to be used formatively, that is provide feedback on learning in order to guide subsequent learning and teaching. However, if it is not acted upon, it may stand as a summative record. In contrast, written tests (large-scale or otherwise) can act as formative assessment if their results are used to assist future learning. However, more frequently written tests, particularly national examinations, are seen as summative instruments providing information about final achievements in that phase of education. The current summative assessment system focuses heavily on reliability at the expense of authentic validity. National testing with its attendant marking and administrative strictures is highly reliable, making it as easy as possible to compare performance of different students (and teachers!). Even with the opportunities for coursework assessment across all ages, the format for assessment is predominantly

time-limited written items. The scope for modification of assessment procedures (both formative and summative) depends on political will and
teachers' willingness and ability to engage in more creative teaching and
assessment practices. If formative assessment methods mirror current national
summative assessment then students can be well prepared for the examinations, but the advantages of authentic assessment are often denied. Working
from the other perspective, developing summative assessment which can
mirror the best features of authentic formative assessment may assist both
assessment practice and learning outcomes. Authentic assessment and evaluation through formal written tests, the most used summative assessment
method, can be contrasted (Table 3.1).

Table 3.1   Authentic and large-scale written assessment contrasted

Authentic assessment	Large scale written test
Gives a true measure of capabilities in a realistic situation	Gives a measure of ability on particular skills in a contrived situation
Tends to be holistic, that is brings together different skills and understanding of contexts	Tends to be atomistic – each question focusing on specific skill/content
Can have high validity	Has limited validity of real context
High reliability can be difficult to achieve	Can have high reliability

Importantly, as Black and Wiliam (1998) argue, students need to be aware
of the intended learning goals and involved in evaluation of their own
learning.

> What this amounts to is that self-assessment by pupils, far from being
> a luxury, is in fact an essential component of formative assessment.
> Where anyone is trying to learn, feedback about their efforts has three
> elements – the *desired goal*, the evidence about their *present position*
> and some understanding of a *way to close the gap* between the two
> (Sadler 1986). All three must to a degree be understood by anyone
> before they can take action to improve their learning.
>
> (Black and Wiliam 1998: 7 (authors' italics))

The first step in implementing effective self- and peer-assessment (and learning), then, is to be clear and explicit about the learning goals we, as teachers,
are trying to achieve. As we have implied, this may represent a challenge given
the multiplicity of possible learning goals and lack of large-scale evidence
about students' development in understanding socio-scientific issues to guide
our choice. However, we offer some examples of assessment trials in order to
consider specific learning goals.

Examples of assessment methods

What we offer here is not a systematic, rigorous collection of assessment methods and outcomes in relation to all the learning goals identified. At present, as with our understanding of the processes and outcomes of citizenship education (Chapter 2, page 23), we do not have a wide and detailed evidence base of achievement outcomes from students in compulsory education. Rather what we offer is exemplification of the issues and problems in assessment through the trialling of a limited number of assessment approaches which concentrate on reasoning and evidence evaluation. Most of these give an indication of what students demonstrate without having had benefits of targeted teaching. The results may give some indication of students' ability and suitable learning strategies. We do not discuss the assessment of understanding of science concepts.

We will begin by discussing examples of evaluation of learning goals at an atomistic level. In principle it may be possible to devise test items or written learning tasks for all the learning goals (page 40). With authentic assessment in mind, we consider procedural knowledge and attitudes and beliefs best evaluated in situations where skills can be fully demonstrated. In some cases this requires a feature not supported by written assessment, for example interaction with others and interaction with extensive data. We thus distinguish between two main extremes of assessment method – written, time-limited *formal test items*, capable of being administered to large numbers of individuals under test conditions; and *classroom activity* in which the activity is identical to a 'normal' learning activity but the focus is on exploring the students' achievements. These extremes can become blurred – we can use formal test items in a learning context, for example. All assessment methods need to have clear mark schemes or assessment criteria in order to clarify the validity and reliability of their use. We have collected research evidence relating to a number of the identified learning goals, related assessment methods and possible learning strategies, but by no means all. Table 3.2 shows those assessment methods for which we can discuss fully evaluated examples. This table also maps learning goals against some *possible* learning strategies which are discussed in the next chapter. In the remainder of this chapter we will generally focus on formal test items, leaving some discussion of class activities to Chapters 5 to 8.

Evaluation of procedural understanding

Decision-making items

The first items we explore are some which address procedural understanding of evidence-based decision-making and cost-benefit analysis. The items are based

Table 3.2   Learning goals, learning strategies and assessment methods – evaluated techniques

Learning goal	Learning strategy	Assessment method
Conceptual knowledge		
Understanding of scientific endeavour	Use of media reports	Formal test item, classroom task
Understanding of probability and risk	Risk analysis	
Recognition of scope of the issue	Community project; media reports	
Sustainable development	Community project	
Procedural knowledge		
Decision-making using evidence	Decision-making task	Formal test item, classroom task
Cost-benefit analysis	Risk-benefit analysis	Formal test item, classroom task
Evidence evaluation, including media reports	Use of media reports	Formal test item, classroom task
Ethical reasoning	Ethical analysis	Classroom task
Attitudes and beliefs		
Clarification of personal and societal values	Ethical analysis; decision-making task	
Recognition of values impinging on issues	Ethical analysis; decision-making task	Classroom task

on those developed for evaluating an innovative course for 12- to 13-year-olds in the US – 'Issues, Evidence and You' by the Science for Public Understanding Program (SEPUP) (Wilson and Draney 1997). One of these items (Box 3.1A) was developed to evaluate students' procedural understanding – in this case skills in *evidence and tradeoffs (ET)* – 'identifying objective scientific evidence as well as evaluating the advantages and disadvantages of different possible solutions to a problem based on the available evidence'. The other two items (Box 3.1B and C) were developed from the structure of the first. The 'pesticide' item (Box 3.1B) was evaluated with 15-year-olds in five schools in England. The third item on 'chemicals in toys' (Box 3.1 C) was developed as part of a research project to trial assessment suitable for assessing aspects of 'scientific enquiry' in the science National Curriculum in England (Osborne and Ratcliffe 2002).

In the SEPUP system, the Evidence and Tradeoffs assessment variable has two elements: Using Evidence and Using Evidence to Make Tradeoffs. The

Box 3.1   Items developed to assess procedural knowledge of evidence-based
            societal decision-making

A Treatment of drinking water (from Koker 1996)

Many countries add chlorine to their drinking water. Scientists know that chlorine kills germs that can cause disease, and reduces death or illness due to unsafe water. How serious is the problem? In countries with untreated water, up to a quarter of the hospital beds are occupied by someone with a water-related illness. Many thousands die as a result.

Scientists also know chlorine can react with other chemicals in the water to form new chemicals that may cause cancer. It is a small but significant risk, and some people are concerned about it.

Which of the following describes the most important issue to consider in deciding whether to put chlorine in drinking water? *Choose one*

A   Reducing the risk of getting cancer from chlorine in the drinking water
B   Preventing the spread of germs in the drinking water
C   Comparing the risk of getting cancer from chlorine in the drinking water with the risk of germs in the water
D   Drinking water that is not contaminated with chemicals
E   I don't know

Choice _____

Explain your answer as fully as you can.

B Pesticides – useful but reactive chemicals

Methyl bromide is a gas and a useful pesticide. It also reacts with ozone and is possibly contributing to depletion of the ozone layer.

Pesticides kill living cells in unwanted plants and animals.
If too little pesticide is used on crops, the yields are low. Also, our health can suffer through eating disease-ridden food.
If too much pesticide is used, residues (unreacted pesticide) can get into the food chain. This can cause cell damage to other plants and animals.

Methyl bromide stops insects and fungi damaging harvested crops, such as rice, coffee, tea and potatoes. Farmers use methyl bromide to remove pests from the soil before growing salad crops such as lettuce, celery and tomatoes.

Methyl bromide users are careful to use as little methyl bromide as possible in killing pests. Even so some may stay unreacted and some escapes into the air.

Methyl bromide in the air may reduce the amount of ozone in the ozone layer. The ozone layer screens out most of the ultra-violet light from the sun.

Ultra-violet light damages plant and animal cells. If the ozone in the ozone layer is reduced more ultra-violet light can reach the earth's surface. There is an increased risk of skin cancer where there are higher levels of ultra-violet light.

Should the use of methyl bromide be banned?   Yes/No/I can't decide   Explain your answer

C Chemicals in plastic toys

Chemicals, called phthalates, are added in very small amounts to PVC plastic to make it soft enough to form flexible shapes. In very large amounts, phthalates can cause liver damage and may cause cancer. Babies' teething rings and other toys are made of this PVC plastic. Babies chew teething rings to help stop the pain from teething.

Some Danish scientists are concerned about the level of phthalates in PVC plastic. They tested several types of teething ring for the level of phthalates in them. They did this by shaking the ring in artificial saliva to mimic what might happen in a baby's mouth. They found three types released large amounts of phthalates in this experiment:

Phthalate level in micrograms

Ring A	Ring B	Maximum level allowed in food	Ring C
2200	1000	50	9

The Danish scientists think that these three teething rings A, B and C should not be sold. They have no information on the effect of these teething rings on babies.

Which of the following describes the most important issue to consider in deciding whether to put phthalates in PVC plastic used for toys? Choose one.

A   Making the plastic soft enough to form toys
B   Having no chemicals which may cause harm in the plastic
C   Comparing the risk of damage to babies from using plastic that is not soft with the risk from chemicals which may cause harm
D   I don't know

Choice _____

Explain your answer fully, using as much information from the passage as you can.

SEPUP scoring guide for these shows how criteria are used to evaluate students' use of evidence and their abilities in weighing evidence (Table 3.3). The criteria are based on the idea of a Structure of Observed Learning Outcomes (SOLO). The SOLO taxonomy was devised by Biggs and Collis (1982) as a method of

Table 3.3   SOLO taxonomy and its assessment use (after Biggs and Collis 1982)

SOLO description	SOLO response type	Using Evidence to Make Tradeoffs (SEPUP) (Box 3.1A)	Marking scheme for QCA items (Box 3.1B and 3.1C)
Pre-structural (level 0)	Cue and response often confused. Fails to realize or see the problem. No evidence or information cited	Missing, illegible, or completely lacks reasons and evidence	No mark
Uni-structural (level 1)	One relevant piece of information or evidence is used in the response	States at least one perspective *but* only provides subjective reasons and/or uses inaccurate or irrelevant evidence	Highlights evidence for one side of the issue
Multi-structural (level 2)	More than one relevant piece of evidence is used. If all relevant pieces are used, they are used independently and relationships are not seen or stated	States at least two options *and* provides some objective reasons using some relevant evidence *but* reasons or choices are incomplete and/or part of the evidence is missing; or only one complete and accurate perspective has been provided	Highlights evidence for both sides of the issue
Relational (level 3)	All relevant information is used and the information is related to determine underlying relationships. No external evidence is used	Uses relevant and accurate evidence to weigh the advantages and disadvantages of multiple options and makes a choice supported by the evidence	Highlights evidence on both sides of the issue and indicates how the balance should be determined
Extended abstract (level 4)	All relevant information is used and related and external information is incorporated. Deduction and induction may be present	Accomplishes level 3 *and* goes beyond in some significant way, e.g. suggesting additional evidence beyond the activity that would further influence choices in specific ways, *or* questioning the source, validity and/or quantity of evidence and explaining how it influences choice	Highlights evidence on both sides of the argument, indicates how the balance should be determined. Comments on/points out limitations of the evidence presented

evaluating the quality of learners' responses to a variety of problems across different domains and subjects. The taxonomy is based on levels in a learning cycle making use of Piagetian stages. There are advantages and disadvantages in using such a scheme. A practical advantage is that it provides a clear structure for marking open-ended questions. However, it presupposes a particular hierarchy in development of reasoning skills. In the absence of empirical evidence for how students progress in using evidence and decision-making, this model provides a possible framework for devising mark schemes and for framing learning strategies. Table 3.3 shows the relevant parts of the SOLO taxonomy, the SEPUP version of Evidence and Tradeoffs (used with item Box 3.1A), and a simplified version used with items in Box 3.1B and 3.1C.

Student performance

Before discussing the strengths and weaknesses of items like these, let us look at the performance of different groups. Item A (drinking water) (from Koker 1996) was used with four different populations, one of whom (US 14-year-olds SEPUP) had experienced *Issues, Evidence and You* with its evidence-based reasoning and three of whom had no experience of evidence-based reasoning within their science classes: 15-year-olds in England; 14-year-olds in England; 14-year-olds in the US (non-SEPUP). Items B (pesticide) and C (chemicals in toys) were used in England with classes with no prior experience. Table 3.4 shows the results for these items according to the mark scheme shown in Table 3.3. As might be expected, 15-year-old UK students showed significantly higher levels than 14-year-old UK students on the drinking water item (t-test $p<0.0001$) – neither having had any exposure to consideration of such issues. The most interesting comparison is between the 14-year-old US SEPUP and the other populations. Although the UK 15-year-olds performed better than the 14-year-old SEPUP cohort, the difference was not significant. The SEPUP cohort significantly outperformed the other 14-year-old populations. This does add weight to the SEPUP evaluation which suggested that students who are encouraged to consider socio-scientific issues systematically do develop sound decision-making capabilities (Koker 1996).

The nature of test items

There is some context dependency across these items. According to teacher-estimated levels of science achievement, similar students performed differently on drinking water and chemicals in toys – with higher, but not statistically significant, levels being shown on the chemicals in toys example. UK teachers and science educators commented on the validity of these two items in the trials. Teachers were concerned about the nature of the language used, particularly that in chemicals in toys. For example, they considered the term 'phthalates'

Table 3.4 SOLO levels/marks achieved on decision-making tasks – percentages of each population

Population		Drinking water item (A)										
	N	0	1	2	3	4	N	0	1	2	3	4
US 14-year SEPUP	105	6	21	46	27	0						
US 14-year non-SEPUP	159	16	33	39	12	0						
								Chemicals in toys item (C)				
UK 14-year	169	24	43	18	13	2	171	13	37	24	17	9
								Pesticide item (B)				
UK 15-year	113	4	20	35	37	4	208	1	34	32	31	2

N – number of students in each population. All are from randomly selected classes. The UK populations answering items A and C were selected to be similar in science achievement.

off-putting, perhaps dissuading students with lower reading ages from attempting the question seriously. The issue of authenticity versus feasibility also emerges. Each of these items was designed to present a real problem in appropriate language – yet there are still some unresolved issues. How much unfamiliar context, content and language should be included? Unfamiliar context can prevent students showing their true understanding and capabilities. Our favourite example of inappropriate context is this question:

Explain why the ice cream does not melt quickly in a Baked Alaska.

To be able to answer this question, assessing understanding of air as a thermal insulator, you have to know what a Baked Alaska is. Yet, real socio-scientific issues are going to contain unfamiliar material – assessing how students can apply skills in dealing with unfamiliar contexts is perhaps the point. However, care has to be taken to ensure that the context is not culturally biased or inaccessible, as in the Baked Alaska example. The most important considerations in constructing an item of this type (and using it to promote learning) are identification of an issue that is not obviously polarized towards one viewpoint and presentation of several pieces of evidence relating to two or more different viewpoints.

Table 3.5 Strengths and weaknesses of reasoning items using SOLO-type marking

Strengths	Weaknesses
Framework provides a hierarchical structure for 'objective'/reliable marking	Marking hierarchy is based on one psychological perspective
Question is accessible to wide range of students	Accessibility of context and information can depend on prior experience. Information is selective and can be wordy
Marking is based on the level of reasoning shown rather than the choice made	Takes no account of interaction between evidence and attitudes in our 'real' reasoning
Can mirror real socio-scientific issues	The issue may need to be seen to be finely balanced in practice (i.e. no obvious choice) to elicit reasoning based on both sides of the argument

Reasoning items using SOLO-type marking have some strengths and weaknesses as far as assessing identified learning goals of conceptual and procedural understanding are concerned (Table 3.5).

The thrust of these items has been to explore students' abilities to present arguments, ideally considering evidence for and against a proposal (cost-benefit analysis). Results from this trialling suggest that many 14 to 15-year-olds can identify salient features of socio-scientific issues presented in this way and some will be able to consider both sides of an issue *without explicit teaching*. We suggest that targeted teaching, using evaluation of decision-making scenarios as a learning strategy, will improve students' abilities to undertake reasoned cost-benefit analysis (see Chapters 4 and 7).

Evaluation of evidence is not limited to socio-scientific issues. It is interesting to compare such assessment with similar forms used in the humanities. Are we assessing the same 'skill' of evaluation of evidence across different subject areas? We can make some direct and indirect comparisons. Assessment in the humanities includes evaluation of decision-making and use of evidence. Examples in Boxes 3.2 to 3.4 show the different types of questions posed in specimen exam papers in history, geography and science from the same GCSE examination board. (GCSE is the national examination at 16 for students in England, Wales and Northern Ireland.)

While acknowledging that each of these examples is taken out of context and has a knowledge base associated with it, it is notable that the history and geography examples attempt to recognize answers of increased reasoning and use of evidence. This has echoes of the SOLO taxonomy. It could be argued that the science example attempts something similar, but the qualitative

---

Box 3.2   Example of assessment of evidence in GCSE History (from OCR 2000a)

Students are provided with sources of evidence (documents and pictures).

'In answering questions you are expected to use your knowledge of the topic to help you interpret and evaluate sources, and to explain your answers. Where you are instructed to use a source you must do so, but you may also use any of the other sources which you think are relevant.'

'Q6. Study all the sources. 'Florence Nightingale made her most important contribution to nursing when she was in the Crimea'. How far do these sources support this view? Explain your answer'   [12 marks]

'*Mark scheme*:
Level 1   Answers which do not use Sources   1–3 marks
Level 2   Answers which use Sources to show that Florence Nightingale did good work in the Crimea or elsewhere   4–6 marks
Level 3   Both elements of level 2   7–8 marks
Level 4   As level 3 but also attempts to consider relative importance or whether work at home was based on fame won in Crimea   9–10 marks
Bonus: Up to +2 bonus for valid evaluation of sources (one for each)'

---

development of arguments using evidence is less apparent in the science example. Factual knowledge rather than synthesis of arguments has more emphasis in science examinations than in the humanities. An additional example from the same specimen science paper serves to reinforce this. At the end of a question about genetics, the following is asked without there being any evidence or context in the question:

> Describe the advantages and disadvantages of genetic engineering (5 marks).

This could be interpreted as a very open question in which students synthesize arguments, drawing on their understanding developed during the course, showing a recognition of the social impact. However, the mark scheme appears mechanical:

> Advantages
> Can avoid hereditary defects; introduces new capabilities; makes new crops available
> Disadvantages
> Risk of creating harmful variants; new illnesses; unknown results not quickly apparent

---

Box 3.3 Example of assessment of evidence in GCSE geography (from OCR 2001)

Air pollution from the glass-making industry in St Helens
Students are provided with line graphs of kg of air pollution per tonne of glass made (0–18) against years (1960–95) for sulphur dioxide and nitrogen oxides as nitrogen dioxide.

(Sulphur dioxide line shows steady shallow decline then rapid dip to 1985 followed by slight increase to 1995; nitrogen dioxide line shows steady shallow decline throughout.)

'(i)   Which gas was the main cause of air pollution between 1960 and 1983? [1]
(ii)   How many kilograms of nitrogen dioxide were produced for every tonne of glass made in 1975?   [1]
(iii) Since 1965 the glass-making industry has tried to reduce air pollution. Use evidence from Figure 2d to describe how successful it has been.'   [3]

'*Mark scheme*
(i)   sulphur dioxide
(ii)   8
(iii) *Level 3*   3 marks
     Reduced emissions of both gases particularly sulphur dioxide/especially 1975–85/exception 1985–95 for sulphur dioxide using accurate figures to illustrate (within tolerance of 0.2).
     Level 2   2 marks
     Refers to general reduction of emissions along with other specifics as above without using figures accurately.
     Level 1   1 mark
Simple statement about reduction of emissions or use of figures without any interpretation.'

(Up to 4 marks for valid facts correctly used)
Arguments effectively linked (1 mark)

While it may be unfair to criticize a question which is unlikely to have been trialled, this question and mark scheme does seem typical of approaches to assessment within formal science examinations. There seems a lack of recognition that issues such as genetic engineering are value-laden and have wide social impact. While we may wish students to be able to list advantages and disadvantages of a scientific 'advancement', of greater and lasting value may be the ability to develop reasoned arguments – a skill more apparent in answering the humanities examples. We suggest that the compartmentalization of

---

Box 3.4 Example of assessment of evidence in GCSE science from (OCR 2000b)

'Jupiter orbits the sun in about 11 earth years. The apparent brightness of Jupiter as seen from Earth increases and decreases steadily in a regular cycle which repeats once every 13 months. Two theories have been suggested to explain this.
Theory A: The amount of dust in the Earth's atmosphere changes at different times of the year.
Theory B: The distance to Jupiter changes as the Earth moves round the Sun.
Use the evidence given to explain which of these theories you think is most likely to be correct.   (5 marks)'

'*Mark scheme*
Against dust theory
Cycle is 13 months, not 12.
Changes are steady and regular, dust levels should vary with the weather.
For orbital distance theory
13 months allows one earth orbit and advancement of Jupiter.
Light intensity varies with distance from source   (4 marks)
Allow up to four marks for factual information correctly applied.
Arguments effectively linked   (1 mark)'

---

the secondary curriculum, including the assessment techniques, prevents sharing and development of expertise across teachers and examiners. It also militates against students transferring skills of argumentation and reasoning across different curriculum areas. There is much to be learnt from collaboration of teachers in different disciplines in addressing science and citizenship.

Evaluating conceptual and procedural understanding

Test items relating to media reports

We now turn to other research and items which attempt to explore aspects of conceptual knowledge as well as procedural knowledge – evidence evaluation and media reporting. The conceptual knowledge explored is the understanding of the nature of scientific endeavour (how scientists develop ideas/theories/models; links with systematic data collection; reporting of findings; peer review). As we have indicated, much of our acquaintance with topical socio-scientific issues arises from media reports. What expertise do students show in evaluating media reporting of science? Do they appreciate the limitations of media reports in being able to present an accessible, but often incomplete, picture of scientific endeavour?

We start by considering some Canadian research with undergraduates and high school leavers. Media reports of scientific research present evidence and resulting knowledge claims but may also include important information about the methods, data, social context of the research, and views of other researchers (see for example Box 1.4, page 8 and Boxes 6.1 and 6.3, page 112). Korpan *et al.* (1997) hoped students might recognize such features as significant in science research. They presented 60 psychology undergraduates with four fictitious news briefs, each of the same length (c. 60 words) and structure – researchers report a finding; a general issue is described; an independent group promotes the importance of the finding and arrives at a conclusion. Students were asked to judge the plausibility of the conclusions and identify information they would need to determine whether the conclusion were true. Korpan *et al.* surmised that, if students understood the nature of scientific research, they might seek information about: methodology; data including statistics; links between evidence and theoretical propositions; social context of research; related research; relevance of the research. The different news briefs elicited varying frequencies of requests for the different categories of information, with the highest categories being methodology (52 per cent of students consistently seeking information across all news briefs) and theoretical propositions (28 per cent). Korpan *et al.* were concerned by the low frequency of requests for information about statistical data, social context and consensual processes. Norris and Phillips (1994) argue that how we interpret a report of scientific research depends upon our views of the nature of science and our ability to distinguish between different types of statements, for example statements of method from statements both of observations and causes:

> If, for instance, a reader assumes that scientific statements express uniformly certain knowledge then this belief is likely to cause misinterpretation of statements that carry varying degrees of expressed certainty. Similarly, if a reader assumes that the sole purpose of reports of science is to relay the certain knowledge that has been discovered, then this belief is likely to inhibit sound interpretation of statements made for other purposes.
>
> (Norris and Phillips 1994: 948)

Media reports can have features, such as cultural norms, consistent with scientific endeavour and discourse itself. The purpose of science discourse is 'to conjecture, to relate alternative views, to express doubt, to challenge, to ask questions, and to relate what is not known' (Norris and Phillips 1994: 959). Thus media reports are in stark contrast to most science textbooks in the picture of science they portray.

Norris and Phillips (1994) presented 91 twelfth-grade high school science students (equivalent to Year 13 in the UK) with five actual reports of scientific research chosen from a range of sources – from a popular newspaper to a scientific journal. For each of these they selected statements from the report and asked students to judge the certainty of the statement, its nature and its role in the chain of reasoning of the report. They found that most students recognized observations, descriptions of methods and conclusions as such but most could not recognize justifications, causal statements and statements of evidence as such. Norris and Phillips suggest this may be because justifications, causal statements and evidence are interrelated and are presented that way, whereas statements of observation and method appear independent. Less than half of their sample of students was successful at any of the tasks where they had to recognize the relationships among statements and interpret them in the context of the whole report. Students were also found to attribute more certainty to statements than was warranted.

In a further, related study, students were asked their beliefs about the topic before reading an article and again after reading. For example, one report was about weather and sickness, so students were asked 'Do you believe that weather can make you sick? Why do you say that?' These beliefs were examined again after reading. In most cases, Phillips and Norris (1999) found that students adopted an uncritical approach to the report. 'The majority of students deferred to the reports by readily accepting the statements of the reports and by implicitly trusting the authors. Few students appraised the report against their background beliefs.' The most influential factor in students' judgements seemed to be what the reports said and not whether and why the reports should be believed. Thus the author's stance, which we consider present in media reports, was not picked up by students in this study. Nelkin (1995: 69) argues that 'public beliefs about science and technology tend to correspond with the messages conveyed in the media, though the direction of cause and effect is not clear. Though the media are often blamed for biasing public opinion, journalists claim they are merely reflecting public views.' Nelkin suggests that the influence of the media on beliefs and behaviour varies with the selective interest and experience of readers:

> In areas of science and technology where readers have little direct information or pre-existing knowledge to guide an independent evaluation (e.g. the effects of fluorocarbons on the atmosphere), the press, as the major source of information, defines the reality of the situation for them. But where readers already have an established set of biases (e.g. about the causes of social behaviour), science reporting tends to justify and reinforce these biases. And when the reader has had personal experience (e.g. with workplace risks) or long-term exposure to media coverage (e.g. about environmental problems or dietary risks), the effect of media images is tempered by prior attitudes about the issues.
>
> (Nelkin 1995: 68–9)

If Nelkin's argument is correct, then the challenge in 'science and citizenship' education is to help learners understand the nature of science and science reporting before their biases become too fixed.

We now discuss the performance of 14-year-old students on test items based on authentic media reports (Osborne and Ratcliffe 2002). The items each have a common thread of assessing understanding of the provisional nature of scientific research, although there are different nuances in each of the items. The air pollution item in Figure 3.1 shows how a simpler version of a media report was constructed with questions similar to those explored in the Canadian research. Table 3.6 shows the performance of 171 students from 13 randomly selected schools. This item fulfilled criteria for large-scale assessment designed to distinguish between students in their attainment of understanding of some aspects of media reporting and the nature of scientific research. Most parts of the item showed reasonable facility and good discrimination. The mark scheme takes into account possible different interpretations of the

Table 3.6   Responses to media report item for 14-year-olds (n = 171)

Item Part	Correct response	Percentage correct
a	Conclusion Answers showing understanding: air pollution may have a major impact on the Earth's climate/air pollution reduces rainfall	88
b	Evidence Satellite images of clouds and measurements from satellites	64
c	Certainty of measurements Very certain – measuring instruments are accurate and are probably repeated or fairly certain – there may be an error in some measurements or I can't judge – there's not enough detail given about the measurements	44
d(i)	Certainty of conclusion Uncertain or fairly certain	71
d(ii)	Reasoning Fairly certain – there's some evidence to support his conclusion or uncertain – more evidence needs to be collected to be more certain/he may need to change his theory with more evidence/he shows lack of certainty ('may')	49
e	Additional work Repeating the process; trying different identified variables/ measurements	47

This question is about how scientists work.
John, a climate scientist, saw a report in a journal *Science* in March 2000. He made a summary of it to report to other scientists

---

Air pollution may have a major impact on the Earth's climate.

Daniel Rosenfeld of the Hebrew University in Jerusalem has investigated the effect of air pollution on rainfall. He has found that there is not as much rain as expected in areas downwind of polluting industries. He used satellite images from the Tropical Rainfall Measuring satellite. The satellite images are like photographs of large areas of sky, allowing measurements of areas of cloud in kilometres. Rosenfeld examined and measured clouds downwind of pollution sites. He claims that the satellite data link air pollution to a reduction in rainfall. He suggests a reason for this. It may be that pollution stops tiny droplets of water from joining together to form raindrops. He says 'these results might indicate that human activity may be altering clouds and natural rainfall worldwide.'

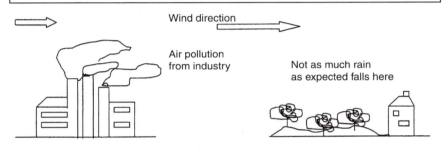

a What conclusion has Daniel Rosenfeld come to from his research?

b What is the evidence Daniel Rosenfeld has for his conclusion?

c How certain can Daniel Rosenfeld be of the measurements from his satellite?
   (i) Ring one of the following:
      Very certain   Fairly certain   Uncertain   I can't judge
   (ii) Explain the reason for your choice

d How certain is Daniel Rosenfeld of his conclusions from examining the data?
   (i) Ring one of the following:
      Very certain   Fairly certain   Uncertain   I can't judge
   (ii) Explain the reason for your choice

e John, the climate scientist who read the original report, wants to do some more research in this area. Describe ONE thing John could do to improve on Daniel Rosenfeld's research.

Figure 3.1   Air pollution: Media report item for 14-year-old students (Osborne and Ratcliffe 2002)

passage and knowledge of satellite imaging. We interpret these results as showing what a random sample of students can do without deliberate teaching (albeit of slightly higher attainment than national performance as shown by teacher estimates). At the risk of generalizing, we postulate that recognizing conclusions, and evidence to support conclusions, is not too difficult. Recognizing limitations of measurements and evidence is more difficult. Thus, in line with Norris and Phillips's (1994) findings, we advocate learning strategies which focus on the strengths and limitations of scientific evidence and its presentation (see Chapters 4 and 6).

Classroom activities relating to media reports

In addition to items for written tests, three longer items for in-class assessment (or teaching) were constructed for use with a variety of age groups (Ratcliffe 1999; Osborne and Ratcliffe 2002). These items each used a media report considered accessible for the age group. An example is shown in Figure 3.2. A number of common questions were asked:

1. Write down one thing in the article which is known for certain.
2. Write down one thing in the article which is uncertain (specified for the third item concerning benzene pollution).
3. Chris has read this article and says
    'This proves that plastic teething rings damage babies' livers' (teething item)
    'This proves that magnets change the chemistry in a swimming pool' (pools item)
    'This proves that people in northern Europe get more benzene in their home than outdoors' (benzene item)
    Do you agree or disagree with Chris?   Explain why you think this.

Each of these items was used in classes of either 12- or 14-year-olds where students completed the tasks unaided, apart from clarification of the language used in the report. Additionally, two of the items, teething and pools, were used under test conditions with 17-year-old students studying at least one science at advanced level and with science graduates training as teachers. Only small numbers undertook this pilot assessment, and with different reports, so it is impossible to generalize to larger populations. However the performance on these items suggests some interesting trends worthy of further study (Table 3.7). It seems easier for most students to identify certainties in reports than uncertainties, although students seem to have more difficulties in a science context (as in the case of benzene pollution). If we take science graduates as people who should show a mature understanding of the nature of this media reporting, then the vast majority of this sample of science graduates can recognize the limitations of either the evidence presented or the nature of reporting. A majority of students can correctly recognize the fallacy of Chris's statement (caveats are presented in the reports) but fewer are able to articulate their reasoning in relation to the evidence presented.

How scientists work

Kevin saw a report in the journal *Nature* in March 2000. He made a summary of it.

Where's the risk – on the street or in your own home?

Benzene can cause cancer. It is found as a gas in car exhausts. Scientists in Italy carried out a large survey in six European towns. The three northern European towns were Antwerp, Copenhagen and Rouen. The three southern European towns were Athens, Murcia and Padua.

They tested for people's exposure to benzene in three ways – outdoors, personal levels and in the home.

They tested for benzene pollution outdoors at 100 sampling sites in each town, using gas samplers from Monday morning to Friday afternoon.

In each town, they tested 50 volunteers and their homes for benzene pollution. 25 of the 50 worked near traffic fumes. 25 of the 50 did not work near traffic.

To test people's personal level of exposure to benzene, each volunteer wore a sampler from Monday morning to Friday afternoon.

To test the level of benzene in the home, the scientists put a sampler in each volunteer's home for the week.

They found that outdoor pollution is greater in southern towns than in northern towns. They think this can be explained by the different weather conditions in the North and South.

In northern towns the benzene pollution in the home was one and a half times the outdoor level. To explain this, the scientists suggest that benzene gas enters the house and is absorbed into the furniture. In northern Europe houses have a lot of soft furnishings such as carpets which can absorb the benzene. Tiling, marble and bare walls are more common in southern Europe.

Because people spend more time inside, at home, than outdoors, the indoor level of benzene is important in the total amount of benzene people get.

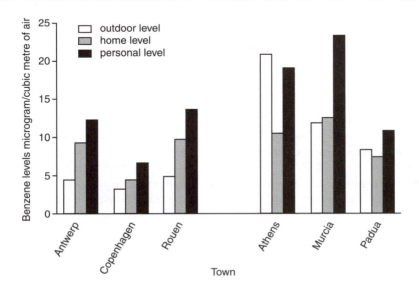

Figure 3.2 Example of media report used in assessment tasks

Table 3.7 Percentage of correct responses to media report task used as teacher assessment

Question	Teething			Pools				Benzene
	Age 12 n=23	Age 17 n=17	Adult n=14	Age 12 n=17	Age 14 n=11	Age 17 n=18	Adult n=15	Age 14 n=29
1 Certainty	96	94	100	77	91	83	93	62
2 Uncertainty	65	71	100	86	82	89	100	55
3a Disagree	78	76	100	64	18	39	73	52
3b Reason	35	53	86	59	0	28	73	21

Context of items

Students were not familiar with answering questions relating to media reports. We are not sure to what extent the context of different reports helps or hinders demonstration of understanding. Presenting items in context in an assessment task raises issues of how teachers 'prepare' pupils for such assessment. We have argued that we want students to develop skills of decision-making, understanding limitations of evidence, linking evidence to conclusions. However, these are learnt in specific contexts according to curricular direction and/or teacher choice. We can either replicate these specific contexts (intentionally or coincidentally) in assessment tasks or use ones that are likely to be unfamiliar. Choosing familiar science contexts in media reports can be seen as assessing recall or easily rehearsed lower level skills, or may be viewed by students as assessing the science content. If we choose unfamiliar contexts in media reports, we have to ensure that the science content is accessible. We summarize what we see as advantages and disadvantages of media report items in Table 3.8.

Table 3.8 Strengths and weaknesses of using media reports in assessment items

Strengths	Weaknesses
Can be used as an authentic context and experience	There may be language and contextual barriers to comprehending the report
Chain of evidence can be explored within a full report	Length of report may raise comprehension and time problems unrelated to understanding of chain of evidence
Questions can be asked about the science concepts as well as the processes of science	If purposes are not articulated clearly students may consider understanding of science concepts as the main aim of the assessment

Assessment through class activities

At one level we see assessment through class activities as indistinguishable from normal learning activities. However, we recognize that if the focus is only on *summative* assessment, for example as coursework for national exams, then teaching does not always address learning deficiencies resulting from these activities. This is shown in our media report class activity above. How could teachers use the results of these items formatively (as 'normal' learning activities)? For example, outcomes from the teacher assessment items on media reports suggest that more direction could be given to students' evaluation of the evidence supporting any conclusion within the reports. The regular evaluation of different reports of scientific research may allow students to recognize the strengths and limitations of media reporting to convey the nuances of scientific endeavour.

Additional examples of class activities are embedded in case studies of learning and teaching presented in later chapters. While we could deal with them discretely here, we consider they are best elucidated within the particular context of each case study. Two case studies focus on conceptual knowledge: nature of scientific endeavour (Chapter 6); sustainability and scope of the issue (Chapter 8). Two consider procedural knowledge: ethical reasoning (Chapter 5); risk-benefit analysis (Chapter 7).

Holistic assessment

Authentic assessment (and learning) of the skills and understanding involved in consideration of socio-scientific issues could be at the holistic level of a student project involving:

- identifying a local issue and considering any national and global connections;
- researching through literature and others' opinions what is already known about the science and views on the issue;
- identifying the nature of 'missing' information;
- carrying out some risk-benefit analysis involving an examination of the feasibility based on scientific evidence;
- evaluating the impact on people/the environment from an ethical point of view;
- suggesting actions based on all these considerations;
- putting the actions into practice.

Students can be encouraged to present their evidence in a variety of forms –

written records, outcomes from group discussion, oral presentations etc. The format of some possible projects is explored in Chapter 4.

Summary

We started this chapter by claiming that exploring assessment methods in relation to the nature of socio-scientific issues would allow us to clarify what is measurable and what is desirable in terms of learning goals. The evidence base we have discussed is partial and biased towards written test items trialled in research. We recognize that there are other items and classroom activities that can be used to evaluate the identified learning goals. For example, the Programme for International Student Assessment (PISA) is assessing scientific literacy through written items (PISA 2002). However, only one minor strand of this – scientific situations – mirrors the learning goals relating to citizenship. Project work and written test items have been features in post-16 'scientific literacy' courses for some considerable time. Development of valid assessment for science education for citizenship in the 5 to 16 age range seems in its infancy.

We have distinguished between two extremes of assessment methods – formal test items and embedded classroom assessment, suggesting that assessment through class activities may promote greater authenticity and validity. We have shown that some atomistic learning goals, relating to conceptual and procedural knowledge, are assessable through written test items. This gives some pointers to development of learning strategies in relation to these discrete goals, particularly conceptual and procedural knowledge. In the next chapter we discuss the nature of learning strategies to address learning goals.

4　Learning strategies

Clarification of learning goals

We have identified in Chapter 3 that some appropriate learning goals may be based on conceptual and procedural knowledge and attitudes and beliefs. So we want students to develop:

- Conceptual knowledge
  - some understanding of scientific endeavour (how scientists develop ideas/theories/models; links with systematic data collection; reporting of findings; peer review);
  - some understanding of probability and risk;
  - recognition of the scope of the issue – personal, local, national, global; political and societal contexts;
  - some understanding of underpinning science concepts; environmental sustainability;
- Procedural knowledge
  - processes of opinion forming/decision-making using a partial and possibly biased information base;
  - evidence evaluation;
  - ethical reasoning;
- Attitudes and beliefs
  - clarification of personal values and ideas of responsibility;
  - interaction of personal and social values.

A particular learning activity may address all three aspects. The 'content' of the activity has some conceptual basis. The task itself engages students in some processes, where involvement and understanding the processes are integral to the learning goals. Inevitably values dimensions are present in the choice of activity, the processes undertaken and the students' viewpoints. The teacher (and students) may manipulate the balance of importance of these three strands in an activity. For example, we may wish to engage students in a discussion about the efficacy of vaccinations against 'flu, and the implications of only small numbers of people being vaccinated. This activity may also involve students identifying whether they would consider being vaccinated. As teachers, we may wish to emphasize the processes of ethical reasoning or decision-making in undertaking this activity. That is, the main purpose would be seen as developing procedural knowledge. We cannot develop procedural knowledge in a vacuum, hence the choice of context such as 'flu vaccination. Equally, the main purpose may be for students to understand the nature, advantages and disadvantages of vaccination – conceptual knowledge. However, it may be impoverishing students if this knowledge is not then used in discussing social aspects. Thus we may have learning outcomes embedded in the *process* of the activity (for example, evidence evaluation; decision-making; ethical reasoning; values clarification) and learning outcomes embedded in the *content* of the activity (for example, understanding of scientific concepts; citizenship concepts; nature of science). How we as teachers see the balance of these learning goals may be different from students' perceptions. It takes considerable clarification between teacher and students to have a mutual understanding of the balance between conceptual and procedural knowledge in discussing socio-scientific issues. For example, when giving emphasis to procedural knowledge, such as understanding ethical analysis and decision-making, we consider it very important to focus on developing the students' quality of reasoning and reflection. Given the multiplicity of possible learning outcomes from consideration of socio-scientific issues, we consider it important to clarify the main purpose from the outset and share this with students. Clarification of learning goals is discussed in more detail in Chapter 5.

Learning strategies

Identification of goals is only one part of considering learning. We also have to consider the nature of appropriate learning strategies and activities when engaging with socio-scientific issues. We believe it difficult for students to progress in identified learning goals without exposing their views to peer and class evaluation in some way.

As a backdrop we examine evidence from a large-scale study, through questionnaire and interview, of headteachers', science teachers', humanities teachers' and personal, social and health education (PSHE) coordinators' views of the teaching of social and ethical aspects of biomedical science (Levinson and Turner 2001). Although most perceived the importance of such teaching, few teachers, particularly of science, were actively engaged in considering socio-scientific issues in their classes. The study found that the most common learning strategies which teachers claimed to use were: discussion (24 per cent); use of videos (7 per cent); debate (4 per cent); group work (3 per cent); role-play (3 per cent). English teachers were the ones most likely to use debate and were enthusiastic of students expressing their views and offering critiques. These are self-reported strategies and we suggest that 'discussion' is open to differing interpretations. Some science teachers may consider whole-class question and answer sessions in which the teacher explores closed questions with accepted answers as discussion. We do not. Rather we consider discussion as an opportunity for students to express their understanding and ideas to other students in a supportive and evaluative environment.

For the purposes of discussing suitable learning approaches dealing with socio-scientific issues, we distinguish between:

A structured learning strategies involving mostly whole-class discussion;
B activities which could be classed as stimuli for analysis and further discussion;
C structured learning strategies supporting small group discussion of socio-scientific issues.

The bulk of this chapter is given to discussing *structured learning activities supporting small group discussion* as we consider these are helpful in developing pedagogical expertise in handling socio-scientific issues. Wellington and Osborne (2001) provide useful examples of discussion activities for exploring scientific evidence (i.e. how we know) as well as science concepts. They also provide guidance on managing discussions.

A Structured learning strategies involving mostly whole-class discussion

Some structured learning strategies, such as role-play and debate, are more suitable for whole-class activity rather than small group work. We consider these of sufficient familiarity to teachers and embedded in many curriculum resources. Role-play can be used to engage students in discussion in a structured and empathetic way. However, we should remember the need for careful debriefing of students after role-play as students may have to argue a position which they have not thought through and which may be very biased in a particular direction. Janis (1968) indicates that such situations, in which people are encouraged to adopt roles in arguing issues, can subsequently affect the view they personally reach.

B   Stimulus activities

Some learning strategies are not so much strategies as stimulus activities for further discussion and analysis. We group these roughly as verbal, visual, multi-media and personal stimuli. For each of these groups we give one or two examples to illustrate their potential in promoting the sharing of views. These activities are useful in starting students thinking but usually require further structure, such as that described in Section C below, to address the identified learning goals fully.

Verbal stimuli (oral or written)

Verbal stimuli include: reading stories or newspaper reports; listening to outside speakers or audio-recordings; mind movies.

Example – mind movies

Mind movies are essentially stories, but students are asked to turn the story into a 'movie' in their minds, by imagining certain 'shots' (Leat 2000). Like stories, they draw on and develop visual memory skills, and they can be especially valuable for work with lower achieving students. They involve the teacher reading a carefully selected passage (taken from a newspaper, magazine, Internet article, etc.) and asking students to imagine the situation. This provides the basis for a class discussion that begins with a deeper feeling for the issue. The strategy requires little preparation, but considerable professional skill, as it is vital to have the students cooperating, trusting and attentive. The teacher does not require particularly good storytelling skills or experiences; this strategy involves reading a 'script', which is a less daunting prospect! After the reading the teacher can ask for suggestions of good movie shots. Students can compare individual images and be asked to choose three shots, each representing an important component of the issue, then describe these shots in writing or orally, or perhaps even as a drawing. For example, if the reading is about people campaigning against incineration of domestic waste, students can be asked to choose shots that represent causes of waste incineration, effects of waste incineration, and action to reduce the problem. They may then start to realize the complexity of the problem.

Visual stimuli

Visual stimuli include: photographs; Internet images; movie stills.

Example – using photographs

One way of using photographs is to uncover an image bit by bit asking students to record their views at each stage (Thorp 1991). For example, you can find an arresting image relating to the issue to be discussed and cover this with a 'cropping card' which leaves only a small area visible. Students, in small groups, are asked to discuss what they think the image is of. The visible area is enlarged to show rather more of the image and students discuss their views again. This is repeated until the whole photo is uncovered. At this stage, students can discuss their original impressions and compare them with the final image. Class discussion can centre around our preconceptions and ideas about other people and places. Further techniques using photos include writing captions and putting pictures in sequence.

Multi-media stimuli

Multi-media stimuli include: video, movies, web-based and powerpoint presentations.

Example – evaluating the message
The impact a multi-media presentation makes on students depends not only on the way the images are used but also on the soundtrack and commentary. Scientific evidence and the views of scientists are often embedded in a multi-media presentation of a socio-scientific issue. Students need some guidance in recognizing the ways in which images are used and the features of sound scientific research. The list of questions shown in Table 4.1 can be used to help students focus on key features while watching multi-media presentations.

Table 4.1   Science in the media – evaluation questions

What's the message	How do we know?
What point(s) of view is presented in the material?	What scientific evidence is included?
What images are used?	Who collected the scientific evidence?
What language is used?	How was the scientific evidence collected?
What music, if any, is used?	What does the scientific evidence tell us?
How do the images/language/music help to get this point of view across?	What are the limitations of the scientific evidence?
Who gives their views?	
How are they portrayed?	

Personal stimuli

Under this heading we group activities in which students are asked to give an immediate and personal reaction. These include activities such as:

mind-mapping; 'heads and hearts'; critical incidents; 'voting' – initial reactions to an issue.

Example – critical incidents

'Critical incidents' are descriptions of real classroom situations, which can be used as a tool for helping students appreciate and articulate their own views about socio-scientific issues, and those of others. The students are confronted with an example of an incident and asked to respond by saying what they *would* do (a reactive perspective), what they *could* do (a proactive perspective) and what they *should* do (a moral perspective) in this situation. An example of such a critical incident could be:

> *You are on a school trip waiting for a coach. Someone spots a large spider and stamps on it. Someone else is outraged by the incident and asks you to say something.*

How the students respond is a useful, and hopefully realistic, indication of their views on the nature of socio-scientific issues. Students become aware of the moral dilemma that what they *could* and *should* do does not always coincide with what they *would* do. Critical incidents have been used with considerable success by Nott and Wellington (1997) to assist science teachers to convey their beliefs about the nature of science.

Example – heads and hearts

This activity is designed to encourage students to consider the roles that emotional reaction and rational thinking play in their reactions to controversial issues. Students consider their immediate reaction to an issue which may have up to four choices. Depending on their responses they vote with their feet and move to the relevant part of the room. For example, a question can be posed:

> *Should we have genetic testing for a very serious genetic disorder, in order to eliminate the disorder in future generations?*

The four corners of the room can be designated as: not at all; compulsory for everyone; compulsory for those with the disorder in previous generations; voluntary for those who want to be tested. Some students may want to stand mid-way between corners. Students are then asked to put a hand on their head if they made the decision by thinking rationally about the issue or to put a hand on their heart if it was an immediate emotional response. They may want to put hands on both head and heart. Selected students can be asked to explain their views. The activity can be repeated with different – 'slippery slope' – scenarios which gradually introduce more complexity and further conflicting values – for example, should we have genetic testing to eliminate hereditary baldness? This activity and discussion can be also used prior to ethical reasoning or risk-benefit analysis (see Section C below).

C Structured learning strategies supporting small group discussion

Small group discussion is difficult to embark on without focus and structure. Support of the teacher in assisting procedures and evaluating outcomes is also essential. Many science teachers lack confidence and expertise in handling unstructured, ad hoc, open-ended discussion. English and humanities teachers are happy to engage students in debate and discussion but lack the focus on substantive science. Few teachers include any understanding of risk assessment, any emphasis on rights and responsibilities or any use of ethical enquiry (Levinson and Turner 2001).

In mapping the learning goals discussed in Chapter 3, we focus on the following types of learning strategy which can all have a place in dealing with socio-scientific issues:

1 Ethical analysis (case study in Chapter 5 – ethical reasoning).
2 Evaluation of media reports (case study in Chapter 6 – use of media reports).
3 Risk benefit analysis (case studies in Chapter 7 – decision-making about socio-scientific issues).
4 Projects: citizenship projects; consensus projects; community projects (case study in Chapter 8).

Table 4.2 shows one way in which the identified learning goals map against these four types of learning strategy. Each type of learning activity is open to addressing other learning goals, but we show in Table 4.2 and discuss in the case studies those learning goals which we think can receive the most emphasis in a particular activity.

1 Ethical analysis

We consider ethical analysis as a process which can help students decide on issues of right (good) and wrong (bad) as applied to people and their actions. We draw on the work of an international group to outline two learning strategies which illustrate this emphasis on procedural knowledge. The *Science, Ethics and Education* project funded by ICSU (International Council of Scientific Unions) produced resources for teaching ethical aspects of science to students who were near the end of their formal education (Fullick and Ratcliffe 1996). Drawing on expertise, research and curriculum development

Table 4.2 Learning goals addressed by four types of learning strategy

Learning goal	Ethical analysis	Use of media reports	Risk-benefit analysis	Projects
Conceptual knowledge				
Scientific endeavour		✔		✔
Probability and risk			✔	✓
Scope of the issue		✓	✓	✔
Science concepts	✓	✓	✓	✓
Procedural knowledge				
Decision-making			✔	✔
Evidence evaluation	✓	✔	✓	✓
Ethical reasoning	✔			✓
Attitudes and beliefs				
Clarification of personal values and responsibility	✔		✔	✓
Interaction of personal and social values	✔	✓	✔	✔

✔ key learning goal ✓ subsidiary learning goal

based in the US and UK, the resources intended to provide teachers with the following:

- an overview of ideas of ethical reasoning;
- a range of structured teaching and learning strategies to allow interaction between science content and ethical reasoning;
- case studies of curriculum material across the sciences, in which structured teaching and learning strategies are embedded.

The suggested learning strategies are set within a framework of ethical analysis to include interpretation, analysis and argument, critique and decision-making. The intended learning outcomes emphasize the *process* of ethical analysis rather than the outcome of reaching a decision. Any evaluation of students' learning should be centred around the quality of the analysis rather than any decision made. We outline here two of the suggested learning strategies of 'goals, rights and responsibilities' and consequence mapping.

In examining the impact of socio-scientific issues on people, the 'goals, rights, responsibilities' framework helps students see how different individual viewpoints on an issue may *justifiably* be reached. The problem is presented to students in the form of a case study (real or constructed) involving a number of people in an ethical dilemma.

An example might be members of a family, their friends and their doctor in considering whether their young child should have the MMR vaccination (see also Chapter 1). Using the framework shown in Box 4.1, students consider the goals, rights and responsibilities initially of one person. There is some empathy with the person but no attempt to 'role-play'. Goals, rights and responsibilities may be in conflict in many situations. People may use all three to justify one course of action over another – usually one of them (a goal, right or responsibility) will be given as the most important reason. The intention of using this strategy is to expose the conflict to students and to consider how different legitimate personal opinions may be reached depending on priorities. Students also gain conceptual understanding of goals, rights and responsibilities. Students may want to have their say in terms of making the

---

Box 4.1   Goals, rights and responsibilities – student activity

Goals are something we aim for; they are the consequences we want. In one way of thinking, a 'good' outcome may be judged morally correct regardless of how the goal was achieved.

Rights are things that are due to us. As a human right, a child can expect to be cared for by his family. A legal right is to be able to vote when we are 18. We are said to have a right if we are entitled to a certain kind of treatment, no matter what the consequences.

Responsibilities are the things we owe others – to tell the truth, to keep a promise and to help a friend, for example. Usually, we justify responsibilities by suggesting that sticking to them will achieve a worthy goal or that they are required because of someone's rights.

Responsibilities may be derived from goals or rights but they may conflict with goals, rights or even other responsibilities. We should not be surprised when we find ourselves torn between competing positions when a difficult decision must be made.

Try to identify the goals, rights and responsibilities of one person *in this particular issue.*
Now collect the views from other groups of the goals, rights and responsibilities of the other people affected by the issue.
Now think about the question again: Should . . .?

Record your group's discussion of arguments for and arguments against.

In your arguments – underline any scientific evidence;
                          – put a circle round value judgements.

decision, but the framework allows the teacher to encourage and expect reasoned arguments for a particular decision.

Consequence mapping allows students to explore a realistic 'What if . . .' issue. Students write the proposition in the centre of a page – for example, 'What if methyl bromide was banned?' Students then consider possible primary and secondary consequences of this proposition, adding these to the map. Other groups of students can consider the opposing 'what if' question – for example, 'What if the use of methyl bromide was encouraged?' When they have exhausted the discussion, students can identify some or all of the positive and negative consequences; those which are certain; those which involve a value judgement; and those where scientific evidence has been used. This consequence mapping is then followed by a discussion as to whether students support, oppose or are uncertain about the proposition. In doing this they are encouraged to identify the values they have used in this reasoning; any scientific evidence they have used and its limits; and the judgements they have made.

A sample consequence map on banning methyl bromide, from Carol's lesson discussed in Chapter 5, is shown in Figure 4.1. This is a real example, not an ideal. You may wish to consider the strengths and limitations of the students' map in addressing the methyl bromide problem.

2 Evaluation of media reports

McClune and Jarman (2001) report that use of newspapers is widespread in science classrooms in Northern Ireland – an initial cause for optimism if we want to encourage students to take a critical stance in examining media reports. However, they found that most teachers used science news reports incidentally, either as display material or opportunistically in showing the relevance of science in the media to the topic under study. They classified a third of the teachers in their survey as systematic users of newspaper reports with 22 per cent being proactive – that is, seeking out articles with deliberate teaching in mind. Science teachers may be willing to use media reports but only 4 per cent of teachers in their sample had critical evaluation of the reports as a potential learning goal. McClune and Jarman suggest that support and direction is needed to help science teachers exploit the potential of media reports in examining both the nature of scientific endeavour and the way in which it is presented.

Students can explore media reports of socio-scientific issues in a number of different ways depending on the particular learning goals identified. A first step in considering media reporting can be to focus on the features, opportunities and constraints presented by different types of media – print media; radio; TV; Internet etc. The Pupil Researcher Initiative (PRI, 2001) provides one unit in which students go through the process of producing a science-based media report for themselves. In doing so they explore features which hook the reader

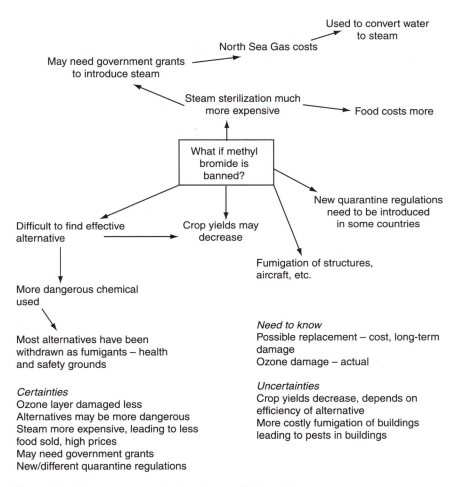

Figure 4.1 Consequence map for banning methyl bromide

– emotions; surprising life-changing events; important new findings; visual presentation. By concentrating on these and other features, such as the role of editors, students can gain more insight into the nature of media-reporting itself. Like many of the strategies we discuss, learning is enhanced if students are engaged in reflection on the processes involved – in this case the extent to which features of media reporting influence people's opinions.

Conceptual understanding of the nature of scientific research

Students can be encouraged to collect reports of science stories from the papers and magazines they read. The reports can then be used to highlight and discuss the features (or lack of them) of the conduct of science. The Science for Public

Understanding course for post–16 students has a useful 'scoring' system for evaluating the expertise of scientists, which could be adapted to apply to media reports (Hunt and Millar 2000: 226). Features of scientific expertise include:

- The theoretical ideas involved – are they established science; several competing explanations; or a fringe theory?
- Nature of the data – are the data reliable and agreed experimental or observational data; sketchy and uncertain; or little more than an educated guess?
- Status of the scientists – are they recognized authorities in this field; respectable but with expertise in a different field; or a known maverick?
- The scientists' institution – do they work for a famous university, scientific research institute or major company; an institution or company which few have heard of; or are they not employed in an academic or scientific research institution?
- Personal affiliation – do the scientists work for an official regulatory body with responsibility for this area; have they been involved in these issues for some time and are known to hold a particular view; or do they work for a company with a direct interest in the issues?

Another way of evaluating media reports is to encourage students to explore them in depth.

In developing conceptual understanding, we could link with learning goals embedded in students' own investigations and enable students to:

- distinguish between results and conclusions;
- identify levels of certainty in drawing conclusions;
- understand how to draw a conclusion consistent with the evidence and relate this to scientific knowledge and understanding;
- comment on the reliability of the evidence, suggesting whether the evidence is sufficient to support a firm conclusion;
- propose improvements, or further work, to provide additional evidence.

The third learning goal in the list also incorporates procedural knowledge.

Authentic research reports that give a potted summary of the research process and output, such as those in the popular science journal *New Scientist*, are useful for this activity. (For example, see Boxes 6.1 and 6.3 in Chapter 6.)

For the case study shown in Chapter 6 the following questions for students were developed in relation to the learning goals above:

- What do the researchers claim (i.e. what is the conclusion)?
- What evidence is there to support this conclusion?

- Is this evidence sufficient to support their claims? Explain your answer.
- What further work, if any, would you suggest?
- What scientific knowledge have the researchers used in *explaining* their results and claims?

These questions have similarity with the expectations on students when evaluating the outcomes of their own investigative work. A refinement of these questions may allow a clearer focus on aspects of scientists' affiliation, team work and peer review as well as evidence and theories:

- Who has done the research?
- What is their conclusion from the research?
- What evidence do they have for their conclusion?
- What theories or models are they using to explain their evidence?
- How certain are the scientists of their conclusions? Do other scientists agree with their findings?

The lessons in the case study in Chapter 6 follow a general structure with teachers using the first set of questions, even when they brought their individual style to bear:

- The teacher presents the report as one intended for an adult audience.
- At some point in the lesson reference is made to evaluation in the context of students' own investigations.
- Students read the report, generally as a whole class. The teacher explores difficulties with terminology either during the reading or subsequently.
- Students then complete the questions in peer group discussion with the teacher circulating to help. The nature of the questions can be explored before the students answer them.
- The teacher leads a class discussion on the answers to the questions, possibly giving discussion time to methods of improving confidence in the research.

Teacher actions and student learning in relation to this strategy are explored in Chapter 6.

3 Risk-benefit analysis

Probability and risk
Good risk analysis involves some understanding of probability and recognition that no activities are risk-free. We may perceive lower risk in a voluntary activity (where we have some control) than in an involuntary activity.

Students can be asked to consider the extent to which they are prepared to engage in a potentially dangerous activity and then compare their perceptions with risk statistics. Figure 4.2, for example, is a student activity of this kind. It aims to give students an introduction to risk statistics, allowing discussion of

Which of the following activities would you be prepared to do every day for a year? (Assume that you had plenty of time and did not have to pay for the activity)

How willing are you to do each activity?

A	B	C	D	E
Willingly	Only if paid £5	Only if paid £50	Only if paid £500	Not at all

Travel 500 miles in passenger aeroplane   Rock climb for an hour
Travel 150 miles in a helicopter   Ski for an hour
Travel 50 miles by rail   Play football for an hour
Travel 50 miles by car   Smoke cigarettes for an hour
Be a motorcycle passenger for 50 miles

Try to decide which three activities would give the greatest risk of death and which three would be the safest – give the least risk of death.

Compare your views with the death statistics table. this information is collected from statistics relating to actual deaths. From this type of information, the likelihood of death in future from the activity can be estimated.

Risk from death of various activities in the UK
Number of deaths per billion hours of the people involved

Rock climbing	40,000
Motorcycle racing	35,000
Travel by helicopter	5,000
Skiing	900
Policeman in Northern Ireland	700
Construction workers on high building	700
Smoking – average	400
Travel by air	400
Travel by car	300
School/college football	300
Oil and gas extraction	150
Average man in his 30s by accident	80
Average man in his 30s from disease	80
Travel by train	50
Factory work	40
Accident at home – all ages	40
Accident at home – able bodied	10
Terrorist bomb in London area	0.1
Building falling down	0.02

Statistics from the British Medical Association (1990); Royal Society (1992)

One billion is 1,000,000,000 (a very large number). The world population is about 5.5 billion. One billion seconds amounts to nearly 32 years!

Figure 4.2   RISKY? Student activity

how these are derived and the nature of voluntary and involuntary risk. Activities like this can be a precursor to discussing:

- science news as presented in the media – why scientists are unable to state categorically the extent of risk associated with eating beef; use of mobile phones etc.;
- how we decide to engage in any particular activity; how, or if at all, we weigh up the risks and benefits involved;
- health-related issues, particularly voluntary risks of smoking.

Decision-making frameworks

One way to structure risk-benefit discussions is to provide students with a decision-making framework to help them to consider options critically and systematically.

There are two different perspectives in the research literature on decision-making:

Normative decision-making models attempt to provide a structure for how decisions *should* be made (for example Beyth-Marom *et al.*, 1991: 26). Researchers using a normative model consider that, if the model were followed, rational, informed decision-making would result. The fit of the models is explored through research which examines deviations in practice from these models and possible reasons for them. There are numerous studies exploring the nature and extent of these deficiencies (for example, Baron and Brown 1991: 95; Swets 1991: 273).

Descriptive decision-making frameworks attempt to provide models, both theoretical and empirical, which describe how real decision-making happens (for example, Hirokawa and Scheerhorn 1986).

A possible decision-making framework with six steps (Box 4.2) was used in the case studies in Chapter 7. In presenting this to students, it was anticipated that they might not follow this slavishly, but that their discussion might be informed by these elements. In other words, the framework might help structure a decision-making discussion without being used in an over-prescriptive way. This framework can be customized for any particular problem. Students may have the greatest ownership and participation if they are able to identify the problem for themselves.

Analysis of others' decisions

Using a decision-making framework allows pupils to consider their views and compare them with those of their peers. The quality of this discussion can depend on students' abilities to generate reasoned arguments. This is a skill that needs support. One way to help students to recognize strengths and weaknesses in reasoning is for them to evaluate the decisions of others. For example, the decision-making assessment item on 'chemicals in toys' (Box

---

Box 4.2   Decision-making framework

Options
> Make a list of all the things you could do/think of relevant to the problem.
> *This statement is phrased appropriately for each different problem.*

Criteria
> How are you going to choose between these options?
> Make a list of the *important* things to think about when you look at each option.

Information
> Do you have useful information about each option?
> What do you know about each alternative in relation to your criteria?
> What information do you have about the science involved?

Survey
> What are the good things about each option?
>   – think about your criteria.
> What are the bad things about each option?
>   – think about your criteria.

Choice
> Which option do you choose?

Review
> What do you think of the decision you have made?
> How could you improve *the way* you made the decision?

3.1C, page 48) can be turned into a learning activity to explore the nature of clear reasoning. A variety of responses to this item can be constructed, or responses collected from one group of students can be used with another. Students can be presented with these responses and asked to identify what they feel makes balanced, or biased, or irrelevant, or well-supported arguments.

4 Projects

The learning strategies discussed so far emphasize specific learning goals and do not attempt to explore the totality of the features of a socio-scientific issue. Perhaps the ultimate strategy is to allow students to undertake a project addressing all learning goals. As indicated in Chapter 3, page 63, the project could be used to support holistic achievement. There has been little evaluation of project work in relation to socio-scientific issues, particularly within compulsory education. We outline some possible approaches.

Study of a topical scientific issue

Project work has been established in post–16 courses which deal with scientific advancements. Early courses such as SISCON (Science in a Social Context) (Addinell and Solomon 1983) and Science in Society (1981) pioneered the study of topical scientific issues, encouraging students to research, discuss and evaluate socio-scientific issues. Latterly, the revision of the post-compulsory curriculum in England and Wales allowed the development of an AS (advanced subsidiary) course in Science for Public Understanding (AQA 1999). As part of this course students undertake two independent projects, one being an account of critical reading of popular scientific writing, the other a study of a topical scientific issue of the student's choosing. Students research, present and evaluate findings in a 2000-word report of a topical issue. While this project does not explicitly tackle all the learning goals that we have identified in relation to socio-scientific issues, it does expect students to address conceptual knowledge, procedural knowledge, attitudes and beliefs. Students are evaluated against the following learning goals:

- Research skills (procedural knowledge) – finding relevant sources, discriminating between them and assessing their reliability.
- Presentation of findings (conceptual and procedural knowledge) – presenting balanced and in-depth coverage of the science relevant to the issue; well-organized presentation.
- Evaluation (conceptual, procedural knowledge, attitudes and beliefs) – reviewing evidence from alternative points of view, including justifying a personal viewpoint; showing good understanding of science knowledge and ideas about science.

Citizenship projects

The introduction of GCSE courses in citizenship provides an opportunity to address socio-scientific issues within the citizenship activity which students undertake as part of the course (AQA 2001; Edexcel, 2001). Although the activity does not have to be science-based, there is a match between some of the expectations of this activity and the learning goals we have outlined. Within GCSE citizenship courses, students are expected to develop:

- knowledge and understanding of events of current interest; roles, rights and responsibilities (conceptual knowledge);
- skills in interpreting different kinds of information, including from the media (procedural knowledge);
- ability to analyse and present evidence on a variety of issues, problems and events (procedural knowledge);
- ability to form and express an opinion in writing (attitudes and beliefs).

Using a scientific or environmental issue to develop these skills and understanding is coincident with our suggestions for learning goals for considering socio-scientific issues.

Consensus projects

A consensus project is an idea suggested by Kolstoe (2000), stemming from his research on exploring Norwegian students' views on socio-scientific issues. The consensus project mirrors a consensus conference, an established method for allowing lay citizens to explore an issue of public concern by hearing and considering the views of various experts. Public reports are produced as a result of consensus conferences, which are becoming increasingly common, particularly in Scandinavia.

In a consensus project students gather knowledge, evidence and opinions on a socio-scientific issue and evaluate what they have found. A difference between this and the other project work described above is that the students act corporately as a class rather than as individuals. The students are divided into different 'expert groups' and one 'lay group'. The class as a whole decide which questions or aspects of the socio-scientific issue are important to explore.

For example, if the socio-scientific issue were 'Should there be continued use of an ozone-depleting pesticide?' then particular questions to explore might be:

How effective is this pesticide?
What is the range of its current use – types and countries?
What health issues are associated with use of different pesticides?
What industry-related issues are associated with use of this pesticide?
What evidence is there for ozone depletion?

Each expert group is expected to gather information from a number of sources on one aspect of the socio-scientific issue in depth, providing evidence to the 'lay group'. While the expert groups are collecting evidence, the 'lay group' decides questions to which they feel they need answers before they can make up their minds – that is, reach consensus on the issue. Each 'expert group' presents evidence and responds to questions from the 'lay group' and from others. When the 'lay group' has heard all the evidence, they discuss what they have heard and try to reach a conclusion. The consensus discussion is held before the whole class, with the 'lay group' articulating their reasons for consensus (or disagreements if these persist) and the 'expert groups' being able to ensure that all their evidence is considered. As Kolstoe indicates (2000: 657), the demands on the teacher and students are high in following the process effectively and fairly. The teacher has to exemplify, through taking part, what critical evidence seeking and good questions to the expert groups might look like. With practice, consensus projects could be a useful way of exploring all learning goals in relation to socio-scientific issues.

Community or cross-curricular projects

The strength of a community or cross-curricular project is in tackling a real and locally relevant issue. Such projects not only bring school and community together, but can also help to bridge the gap between science in the classroom and science in 'everyday life', and show how science links with aspects of citizenship. If the issue is to be explored fully and authentically, the parties involved must collaborate through partnership. Chapter 8 describes and evaluates a collaborative community project focusing on sustainable development.

Much has been written about the virtues of community education, building on research findings that educational participation among children and adults is strongly connected with the extent of an individual's integration into community life (McGivney 1993). Community education is about the creation of opportunities for community members – individuals, schools, businesses, and public and private organizations – to become partners in addressing community needs. Many non-governmental organizations have a programme of community-based projects encouraging schools to take part in local community work. However, schools themselves are seldom proactive in initiating such working partnerships – that is, working *with* the local community, rather than for them, or on them! Community projects, such as the one discussed in Chapter 8, aim to deliver science curriculum requirements by using familiar local socio-scientific issues, often coloured by the unique features and personalities of the local community. Such approaches emanate from the belief that student learning will benefit if teachers, employers and other members of the local community gradually come to appreciate each other's expectations. Science teachers can begin to enhance their classroom work by using local resources and illustrations drawn from their knowledge of the local surroundings.

The case study in Chapter 8 focuses on practical aspects of building and sustaining a local community collaborative partnership, looking at interactions between teachers and the other community participants. Constructive outcomes of this nature may well have a positive impact on children's learning.

To address holistically the learning goals related to socio-scientific issues, a community or cross-curricular project can take the following form:

- establish in collaboration with students and community groups the nature of a local problem or issue;
- seek students' views on the issue – initially these are likely to be uninformed;
- allow students to investigate the issue by engagement with it in the community, and by collecting and evaluating relevant data – first- or second-hand;

- allow students to explore the views of different groups involved in the issue;
- students can then evaluate the data alongside their views and those of others to suggest a way forward with the issue.

While they may not have the skills, knowledge and understanding to resolve a real community problem, students' engagement can allow them to appreciate the complexity of the issue and the nature of differing viewpoints in considering evidence. Through this direct participation, students can provide the community with new insights.

Implementation of learning strategies – case studies

As indicated, the implementation of some learning strategies is examined in detail in Chapters 5 to 8. These case study chapters each focus on particular learning goals and aspects of socio-scientific issues.

In most of these case studies, the students were aged 13–15. Adolescents were usually chosen for this research because students of this age:

- have a substantial science curriculum experience behind them. They might be expected to be familiar with or have an adequate understanding of some of the scientific concepts needed;
- may still be forming their opinions regarding social issues. They may be mature enough to appreciate some of the complexities of real decision-making but are unlikely to be sufficiently informed or prejudiced to have made real commitment to particular ideologies.

The four case studies in brief are:

Ethical reasoning (Chapter 5)
This example features a teacher introducing ethical aspects of science into mainstream chemistry lessons.
The main issues we emphasize are:
- learning outcomes related to procedural knowledge of ethical analysis;
- clarification of learning goals – perceptions of students and teacher.

Use of media reports (Chapter 6)
This case study explores how a science department of six teachers attempted to introduce media reports into a new scheme of work for 15-year-old students.

The main issues we emphasize are:
- teacher change in implementing new learning strategies;
- learning outcomes related to conceptual knowledge of scientific endeavour.

Decision-making about socio-scientific issues (Chapter 7)
We start with an exploration of 15-year-old students discussing conservation of different animals in considering aspects of sustainability. These discussions are undertaken without teacher support. In contrast, we then examine a year-long study of 15-year-old students undertaking decision-making tasks as a regular feature of their science course.
The main issues we emphasize are:
- learning outcomes – procedural knowledge of decision-making, values clarification;
- teacher role in chairing, facilitating and summarizing peer group discussions.

Conceptual knowledge and use of relevant science concepts feature as a sub-issue.

Community projects (Chapter 8)
This case study follows primary and secondary science teachers and their pupils as they work together on a local environmental education project.
The main issues we emphasize are:
- teacher collaboration – the issues and outcomes from working with others;
- learning strategies – conceptual knowledge of scope of the issue; sustainability.

Implementing learning strategies – issues for the teacher

For the teacher, implementation of appropriate learning strategies involves:

- clarification of the learning goals for the particular activity;
- consideration of the structure of the task;
- clarification of the role the teacher should take in introducing, facilitating and summarizing values-based discussions;
- monitoring progress in learning.

A key consideration for teachers is how to chair and manage discussions on controversial issues. The statutory requirements of the 1996 Education Act in England aim to ensure that students are not presented with only one side of political or controversial issues by teachers. In particular, teachers are required to take all reasonable practical steps to ensure that, where political or controversial issues are brought to students' attention, they offer a balanced presentation or opposing views.

The initial guidance on enacting the citizenship curriculum in schools in England indicates how teachers might be expected to behave to comply with these requirements:

> Experienced teachers will seek to avoid bias by resisting any inclination to:
> - highlight a particular selection of facts or items of evidence thereby giving them a greater importance than other equally relevant information;
> - present information as if it is not open to alternative interpretation or qualification or contradiction;
> - set themselves up as the sole authority not only on matters of 'fact' but also on matters of opinion;
> - present opinions and other value judgements as if they are facts;
> - give their own accounts of the views of others instead of using the actual claims and assertions as expressed by various interest groups themselves;
> - reveal their own preferences by facial expressions, gestures, tone of voice etc.;
> - imply preferences by a particular choice of respondents or by not opening up opportunities for all students to contribute their views to a discussion;
> - neglect challenging a consensus of opinion which emerges too readily.
>
> (QCA 2000: 35)

Given this list and the unfamiliarity of most science teachers with discussion of controversial issues, it is unsurprising that many teachers are reticent about discussing topical issues with students. The Crick Report (Advisory Group on Citizenship 1998: 59) acknowledges three general approaches adopted by teachers in handling controversial issues: a 'neutral chair', a 'balanced' and a 'stated commitment' approach.

The 'neutral chair' approach stems from the Schools Council Humanities Curriculum Project (HCP) (Stenhouse 1970). In this role the teacher acts as facilitator in encouraging students to explore the issue and express their opinions fully. Teachers do not declare their own view. The basis for procedural neutrality led from beliefs of the HCP development team of the importance of: educational values of rationality, readiness to listen to views of others; the maintenance of teacher's procedural authority but renouncing authority as the 'expert' capable of solving value issues; avoidance of indoctrination with the main aim as understanding and not forming a premature decision (Rudduck 1986: 11).

The 'balanced' approach assumes that teachers will ensure that all different aspects and views are covered. They will discourage discussions which only concentrate on one particular viewpoint, acting as 'devil's advocate', if necessary, to counter one-sided arguments.

In the 'stated commitment' approach, the teacher declares his or her own views at the outset, encouraging students to disagree or agree on the basis of their reasoning.

Each of these three perspectives suffers from advantages and disadvantages. The 'stated commitment' approach allows students to recognize teachers as individuals with their own perspectives on an issue, yet 'carries the risk that teachers who use it may well be accused of bias and attempting to indoctrinate those whom they are teaching' (Advisory Group on Citizenship 1998: 59). The reality that teachers hold views is ignored in the 'neutral chair' and 'balanced' approach, despite encouraging open discussion. The plurality of views encouraged by both these approaches may prevent students from developing critical skills to judge the worth and validity of different solutions. In Chapter 7 we explore the strengths and limitations of these approaches in practice through examining the actions of two teachers.

Reading the previous section may discourage any teacher from embarking on discussion of controversial issues, particular if they are encountering unknown territory. However, using common sense in dealing with issues in practice – a stance encouraged by the Crick Report (Advisory Group on Citizenship 1998: 60) – should dispel fears of indoctrination and insensitivity.

We have ordered the case study chapters according to the extent of teacher change or innovation. Thus in Chapter 5 (ethical reasoning) we consider how one teacher modified her practice on a small scale – where clarification of learning goals became important. In Chapters 6 and 7 we explore how teachers in two science departments reacted to a larger scale innovation – systematically using media reports (Chapter 6) or decision-making tasks (Chapter 7). The focus in Chapter 6 is on the extent to which different teachers adopted an innovation and the implications that curriculum change brings with it. At a more specific level, each teacher has to decide how he or she will handle student-based discussions of socio-scientific issues. In Chapter 7, in discussing the role teachers take in leading, chairing or monitoring discussions we consider the actions of two teachers. Collaboration with other teachers requires a further level of change and negotiation. We have indicated that cross-curricular collaboration may prove beneficial in addressing socio-scientific issues effectively. We believe this also applies to 'cross-phase' collaboration. Thus Chapter 8 focuses on the advantages and issues of teacher collaboration in a cross-phase study, in which primary and secondary school teachers collaborated with other agencies in fieldwork related to socio-scientific issues.

5   Ethical reasoning

In this case study we evaluate the use of learning activities focusing on ethical analysis. In particular, we explore how one teacher and her classes tackled tasks with unfamiliar learning outcomes.

In 1996 an international group produced resources for teaching ethical aspects of science to students who were near the end of their formal education (Fullick and Ratcliffe 1996). Nine case studies were developed to cover a range of scientific topics suitable for such students, with a minimum prior knowledge of the science content assumed. Each case study had learning outcomes which related to:

- understanding some science concepts (conceptual knowledge);
- understanding the complexity of ethical issues;
- processes of judgement forming, evaluation, analysis (procedural knowledge).

Table 5.1 shows a summary of some of the case studies in terms of the focus and learning approach.

Barriers to implementation

A number of issues seem related to the enthusiasm with which teachers approached these curriculum materials:

- their relevance to science teaching issues 'of the moment';
- their immediate applicability to classroom practice;
- their intrinsic interest.

Discussion with teachers suggests that they find ethical aspects of science interesting but not of immediate importance in tackling the major conceptual

Table 5.1 Summary of some case studies in *Teaching Ethical Aspects of Science* (Fullick and Ratcliffe 1996)

Title	Issue	Ethics focus	Science focus	Learning approach	Prior knowledge
Physical science					
Should methyl bromide be used as a pesticide?	Using ozone depletors	Profit vs global responsibility	Ozone chemistry, pesticides	Consequence mapping, cost-benefit analysis	Some chemistry
Conduct of science					
Professional ethics	Professional conduct of science	Utilitarianism and impartiality as ethical principles	Electrochemistry (nuclear fusion as energy source)	Practical, questions, analysis of scientists' conduct	Some chemistry, (nature of nuclear reactions)
Biological science					
Genetics and ethics Goals, rights and duties	Framework for analysing bioethics	Goals, rights and duties – personal and societal	Inherited disease and genetic medicine	Reading; group discussion using structured analysis	Simple genetics

demands of the science curriculum. Only a few enthusiasts consistently use the advocated teaching strategies of coherent analysis. Many attribute their unwillingness/inability to use such teaching strategies to the content-dominated nature of the curriculum and the difficulty of dealing with issues which do not have a simple, correct answer (an issue we examine further in examining one teacher's practice).

The uptake of these curriculum materials was explored through question-naires seeking information as to how *Teaching Ethical Aspects of Science* (Fullick and Ratcliffe 1996) was being used, if at all. Less than 40 per cent of schools who had been given copies were using the resources. Even those institutions using the case studies indicated that they were time-consuming but many saw the introduction to a range of teaching and learning strategies as a positive feature. The case studies were most likely to be used with older and higher achieving students.

Implementation of teaching materials

Against this background of perceived constraints and opportunities within the resources, we explore the actions of Carol, an experienced science teacher. Carol was keen to try some of the case studies and had already used one prior to implementation of 'methyl bromide' and 'professional ethics'. We explore the lessons she undertook on these topics. Carol drew directly on the case studies as presented (summary in Table 5.1). In 'methyl bromide' Carol discussed relevant free-radical chemistry with a small A level chemistry group (16- to 17-year-olds) before asking them to complete two contrasting consequence maps for continuing the use or banning the use of methyl bromide (for an actual example see Figure 4.1, page 75). This led to a class discussion of how the students would make the decision as to whether methyl bromide should be banned. In 'professional ethics', small groups of 15-year-old students were set the task of producing the maximum voltage they could in an electrochemical cell, given access to a variety of metals and within a time limit. One member of each group acted as an observer to report how the 'researchers' conducted themselves (Box 5.1). Class discussion, which followed, was intended to draw out ethical aspects of scientists' conduct. The lessons were audio-taped and students completed a questionnaire exploring their perceptions of the actions of scientists and the lesson activities.

Learning goals

Possible learning goals for these two activities were given in the resources. Each of these learning goals can be mapped against the strands of conceptual knowledge; procedural knowledge; attitudes and beliefs (indicated in Chapter 3).

Box 5.1 Briefing for students on practical work in 'professional ethics'

Researchers
You are part of a research team which is working on the production of electricity. You are trying to find the combination of electrodes which will give the highest voltage in a simple electric cell. Other research teams are also working on the same problem. You have 20 minutes in which to determine the metals you recommend for use in a simple electric cell. You will then present your findings for review by all research teams. Carry out this investigation with your partner in the way in which you think scientists should proceed.

Observer
Watch the two partners carrying out the experiment and record carefully what they do as they carry out their piece of scientific research.
  For example:
- What decisions are made?
- What measurements are made?
- What materials are used?
- How do the two members of the team behave?
- Is there any influence of other research teams?

Methyl bromide
The students will:

- use their knowledge of society and appropriate science to consider the possible outcomes of banning a useful chemical (conceptual knowledge);
- make judgements about the advantages and disadvantages of banning a chemical, through rational analysis of the rights and responsibilities of individuals and groups (procedural knowledge of ethical reasoning; attitudes and beliefs);
- make judgements about the validity of the scientific evidence supporting particular viewpoints (procedural knowledge of evidence evaluation; attitudes and beliefs);
- realize that such issues are complex and that ethical analysis helps in examining the complexity (conceptual knowledge).

Professional ethics
The students will:

- examine their own conduct as scientists in carrying out research (attitudes and beliefs);

- use this experience as a basis for considering the validity of ethical principles, including motives, for doing scientific research (conceptual knowledge of ethical principles);
- consider and make judgements about the conduct of some professional scientists in their research; these judgements will be based on a rational analysis of the actions of scientists, politicians and industrialists (procedural knowledge of ethical reasoning);
- analyse their discussions to reflect on the ethical reasoning involved (procedural knowledge of ethical reasoning; attitudes and beliefs).

Within the outcomes relating to procedural knowledge, and those for attitudes and beliefs, there may be a hierarchy of possible purposes. These relate to Bridges' (1979) considerations of the functions for discussion of controversial issues:

a   sharing individual perspectives – a sufficient goal in itself;
b   reaching an understanding of the variety of available subjective responses;
c   making a choice between differing values;
d   finding a rational resolution of the controversy.

Here, it is useful to examine teacher and student perceptions of the activities in relation to possible learning goals. The discussion with Carol after her first attempt in implementing the 'methyl bromide' case study (Box 5.2) illustrates her struggle to deal with uncertainty and the need she felt for closure (c or d of Bridges' functions). She shows concern at not summarizing an activity in terms normally associated with science lessons, for example a summary of science concepts covered. How bothered should the teacher be about this perceived lack of closure? It may be helpful to examine the students' perceptions of the lesson. The lesson was with a small class (five students). In written responses to 'What did you learn from the lesson?', their learning gains were expressed in two ways: knowledge of methyl bromide as a useful but dangerous chemical (four students) (conceptual knowledge); consideration of advantages and disadvantages of methyl bromide (three students) (procedural knowledge). Three of the five students felt uncomfortable with the same uncertainty as the teacher in experiencing a 'different' science lesson – 'I didn't completely know what was expected of me'; 'I disliked not knowing where the lesson was going'; 'I disliked being asked to classify things without knowing enough.' However, there was unanimity in appreciating the opportunity for group discussion to share perspectives and clarify ideas (attitudes and beliefs). The students were thus fulfilling the first of Bridges' purposes – sharing perspectives. Although this was reinforced in their class discussion with Carol it was perhaps an insufficient goal for Carol and her

---

Box 5.2   Carol's perceptions of difficulties in introducing ethical analysis

---

Interviewer: You said this lesson had difficulties. What did you think they were?

Carol: I think because you don't know what they're going to say – that's one problem. Because really if you taught electricity or electromagnets or whatever a few times you know what pitfalls they're going to drop into or what they're going to say. Whereas if you're teaching something you've never ever done before and you don't know to 100% yourself I think it's a bit concerning that you're not going to know.

I: So one of the things they were saying – on the feedback – one or two of them were saying they weren't sure where the lesson was going.

Carol: Yes, Yes.

I: So what did you think was the purpose of the lesson?

Carol: Um, I suppose to see whether they thought – after discussion – whether methyl bromide should be banned or not – or if they could come to a decision or not and if it was easy to come to those sort of decisions.

I: I'm interested you said that you felt that the objective might be to come to a decision?

Carol: Yeh, I suppose because it's *should* methyl bromide be used as a pesticide I sort of think well perhaps we should we try and sum up in some way and find out a viewpoint. Because I suppose if you're not going to sum up in that way – summing up in another way like how scientists come to conclusions or how things are viewed feels more time-consuming I suppose.

I: The intention of those materials was to help pupils see that all these factors *do* bear on making a decision – and so different groups may legitimately come to different conclusions.

Carol: Yeh I think I probably changed my outcome a bit as I realized I was running out of time. I think if I'd had a bit longer time then I might have done much more about how different groups of people might react – farmers, scientists and so on, and maybe got more of an angle on that, but because of feeling a bit pressurized with time I perhaps came to a bit of a different outcome than I would have done normally, because I felt a bit anxious to sum up in some way – however briefly.

students. However, reflection on the analysis was underexplored, as Carol admitted.

The appreciation of group discussion and opportunities to share ideas with peers was also evident in the 'professional ethics' case study. The vast majority of the 15-year-old students appreciated the heavy individual involvement in the practical activity and discussion. Carol seemed more comfortable with the planning and conduct of this lesson, perhaps because its structure matched a more normal science lesson – introduction, focused practical activity, class discussion. Although the details of what the students would achieve seemed uncertain, the format of dealing with different outcomes from a practical activity is by no means unknown to science teachers. The interesting difference is in the intended class discussion. It was not the 'traditional' one of reaching consensus on 'what science have we learnt from this experiment?' but rather aimed to illustrate the features of how scientists might deal with:

- different research groups having different findings;
- evaluation of evidence;
- publication and peer review;
- traits of scientific conduct – e.g. honesty, experimental rigour, suspension of judgement.

Students' questionnaire responses indicated that learning gains were mostly seen as conceptual knowledge (production of electricity from metals – 60 per cent of students). This suggests similar difficulties to the 'methyl bromide' lesson in student and teacher adaptation to less familiar learning goals. However, some students (33 per cent) did identify procedural knowledge, conduct of scientific investigations, as their learning gain.

Ethical reasoning in action?

In these two lessons – 'Methyl bromide' and 'Professional ethics' – there was whole-class discussion focusing on the outcomes of the student activity. In the discussions ethics was not mentioned specifically by name. Perusal of transcripts might suggest that intentions of making the ethical aspects of science overt had not been realized. However, there were comments by teacher and students about people's actions.

The class discussion in 'Professional ethics' was substantial and gave considerable time to consideration of the students' actions in carrying out and observing the actions of the experimenters. Some features of the discussion related to the conduct of students' scientific research, integrity of scientists, data collection, and extent of consensus in conclusions.

None of the groups seemed curious about what the accepted answer might be for the maximum possible voltage from their different metals. They argued strongly for their own results as being right despite the clear discrepancies between the groups' results. Carol raised questions about what the class could agree on and how consensus amongst scientists might be reached. Some students still argued strongly for their one original observation as correct (citing the teacher as an observer of their highest voltage), even when they then all repeated their experiment in front of the others to try to establish whether the groups' results could be replicated. In practice, replication proved problematic. The ensuing discussion centred on how scientists' results gain credibility – most students argued for data validated by joint observation (video camera, other scientists' observing). Thus, despite ethics not being mentioned by name students were discussing aspects of scientific conduct.

Information-based versus value-based reasoning

We have argued that in dealing with socio-scientific issues, conceptual knowledge and values are intertwined. In the case of the methyl bromide discussion, the students identified further information (conceptual knowledge) they would want to know before reaching a decision. This related principally to the effectiveness of alternative pesticides compared with methyl bromide but, as the students commented, the information base and its interaction with one's own views are important.

> E: You'd need to know all the alternatives and all the pros and cons about them. You'd need to know everything you possibly could so you could get it right because once you've made your decision you couldn't really change your mind.
> J: It depends on your personal views doesn't it?

The latter comment from student J, combined with consequence maps focusing on the scientific context (Figure 4.1, page 75), illustrate some of the clashes of 'social cognition' and 'non-social' cognition in considering socio-scientific issues in science lessons. Students, and Carol, are used to considering just the physical world in science lessons. They are not used to voicing their opinions and engaging in social reasoning. Fleming (1986) carried out a study which explored Canadian students' integration of knowledge of the physical world and knowledge of the social world in addressing socio-scientific issues. He identifies three conceptual domains as the basis of an individual's construction of the social world:

> the psychological domain, which pertains to knowledge of self, identity, and the causes of one's own and others' behaviour; the moral domain, which pertains to concepts of fairness and justice; and the

societal domain, which includes issues of social regulation and social organisation.

(Fleming 1986: 678)

Fleming argues that 'empirical evidence indicates that moral, social-conventional and personal concepts are fundamentally distinct, parallel, and irreducible ways of thinking about the social world.' He refers to knowledge of the physical world as 'non-social' cognition in contrast to the 'social cognition' just described. He argues, from empirical work, that social cognition dominates in reasoning about the issues as opposed to non-social cognition and that teaching materials must be structured in such a way as to stimulate social cognition.

The students who participated in these two lessons completed a questionnaire designed to explore their perceptions of the interaction between science and ethics. In terms of considering the use of science and technology in solving societal and moral problems, the 15-year-old students seemed more likely than the 17-year-olds to consider this from an information perspective (non-social cognition) rather than an interaction with the views of the public at large (social cognition).

On the basis of the observations of Carol's lesson and Fleming's arguments, there could be a sound case for treating socio-scientific issues in lessons other than science – developing social cognition and ethical reasoning. However, we want to suspend judgement on this issue for the moment. We return to the place of socio-scientific issues in the curriculum in Chapter 9.

It is inappropriate from this examination of one teacher's classes to generalize to other populations but it does highlight some features also seen in other cases (Ratcliffe 1997):

- the opportunity for students to reflect on their actions and articulate this reflection is highly valued by students (attitudes and beliefs);
- clarifying and re-emphasizing the purpose of the lesson is important to ensure that the teachers and students understand and sustain the expectations of the lesson outcomes.

In 'professional ethics', Carol emphasized to the students the rather different nature of the lesson from normal in that it was considering scientists' conduct. In the introduction she indicated some of the features of scientific conduct she intended to explore.

Carol: We're going to be looking at the way scientists work . . . I made a list for what sort of things might be crucial for scientists' conduct. Things like being accurate – so things like not just quickly taking a reading of a meter or something like that but making sure it is a proper reading.

Being honest – not lying about your results. Not copying somebody else's. If you make a prediction and you think, 'Right, that's what I think's going to happen – I'm sure that will definitely, definitely happen' and then you're only looking for that then you're not really being very open-minded. You're just perhaps expecting that result to happen, so you might miss results that are a little bit unusual but are real results – so perhaps being open-minded.

However, the intention of exploring these different facets of scientific conduct in the summary class discussion got lost in an extensive discussion of experimental procedures. Because of the long discussion about the reliability of the groups' results, little time was available to relate the students' work to that of real scientists, as intended in the resources. In conversation after the lesson, Carol saw the main value of the discussion as assisting the students in considering the conduct of their subsequent investigations – in contrast to the detail in the introduction to the lesson. Sustaining the intended purposes and focusing class discussion are not easy when faced with other legitimate reactions from students. We suspect both Carol and the students had difficulty adjusting their expectations of a class discussion.

Summary

This case study has shown how one teacher, Carol, embarked on ethical analysis with no previous experience or training. Carol felt that the success of the activities in promoting structured discussion and ethical reasoning had been mixed. The positive aspects were students' willingness and valuing of small group discussion and Carol's developing confidence to repeat such activities, focusing closure on reviewing the process of analysis or ethical principles, rather than science concepts. She felt negative aspects included the extent to which both she and the students felt they had moved away from normal practice. We feel it important to build structured, small group discussion into students' experience from an early age in science in order to overcome expectations of science lessons as having no room for students to voice and share their views – either on ethical principles or 'normal' science concepts.

6 Use of media reports

In this chapter we discuss the impact on teachers and students of modifying lessons to incorporate evaluation of media reports of scientific research. We are particularly interested in the extent of change this represented to the teachers and the students' learning. The setting for the research was a new comprehensive school where Angela had just been appointed as Head of Science. Angela was keen to bring 'up-to-date' science into the GCSE modular science course in its first year of operation in this school. Building on pilot work (Ratcliffe 1999), we planned a way of incorporating media reports of science into each of the seven modules of the first year of the course (15-year-olds). All six teachers in the science department agreed to be actively involved in trying new approaches. However, they considered it very important that any new activity must fulfil course objectives and integrate fully with the schemes of work they were each writing. Each teacher was responsible for planning one or more of the seven modules in the first year of the course (a module lasted for fifteen 100 minute lessons, five weeks). We planned one activity per module and decided to link the study of media reports to the nature of investigations which students themselves undertake – providing an opportunity for students to explore the nature of scientific evidence and its reporting. Although different media reports were used in each module, common intended learning outcomes were identified. These were mainly concerned with conceptual knowledge of scientific processes related to students' own investigations. Intended learning outcomes and suggested learning strategies have been outlined in Chapter 4, page 76. As a reminder, we show the questions posed to students about each media report:

1 What do the researchers claim (i.e. what is the conclusion)?
2 What evidence is there to support this conclusion?
3 Is this evidence sufficient to support their claims? Explain your answer.
4 What further work, if any, would you suggest?

5   What scientific knowledge have the researchers used in *explaining* their results and claims?

Teacher implementation

Each teacher taught the whole science course to one class of about 20 students. The classes were set roughly according to prior achievement, with two parallel 'top' classes (taught by Angela and Bob) and the remaining four mixed. Table 6.1 shows the intended and actual use of these reports by the six teachers. On only a third of the intended occasions were media reports used. We will look at possible reasons for this after considering the occasions where lessons were implemented. Angela, Chloe and Bob each used at least three of the media reports and we concentrate on these three teachers.

A number of methods were used to explore teachers' views and implementation of activities. Teachers' views were collected through audio-taped discussion and individual interview. An initial departmental discussion clarified the intentions and methods of the activities. Much later in the year, the department held a lengthy meeting for reviewing and future planning. Teachers were interviewed individually at the end of the school year to explore their perceptions of: influences on their lesson planning and implementation, including the school's expectations; their aims and ethos in science lessons; and their intended responses to a proposed (hypothetical) curriculum change. Although each of these methods was intended to involve all six teachers, only Angela, Bob, Chloe and Eric were interviewed. Each lesson, in which a media report was used, was audio-taped to gather data on the way in which the teacher

Table 6.1 Intended and actual pattern of use of media reports by different teachers

	Sept		Jan		April		July
Module	1	2	3	4	5	6	7
Teacher							
Angela	**Chem1**	**Phys1**	**Chem2**	Phys2	**Bio2**	Bio1	**Envt**
Bob	**Chem2**	Bio2	Bio1	**Phys1**	Phys2	Chem1	**Envt**
Chloe	**Bio2**	**Bio1***	Phys2	**Chem2***	Chem1	Phys1	**Envt**
Don	**Bio2**	Bio1	Chem1	Phys1	Chem2	Phys2	Envt
Eric	Phys2	**Chem2***	Bio2	Bio1	Phys1	Chem2	Envt
Fran	Phys1	Bio2	Bio1	Chem1	Phys2	Chem2	Envt

Bold text indicates media report used in that module.
Modules were: Bio1 – Maintenance of Life; Bio2 – Humans as organisms; Chem1 – Earth materials; Chem2 – Metals; Phys1 – Energy; Phys2 – Electricity; Envt – Environment.
* shows occasions on which researcher supported delivery of the activity.

introduced, supported and summarized the activity. Field notes were made to record students' activities and reactions, with some audio-taping of group discussion, and student written work was collected.

Actions of individual teachers

Angela, Bob and Chloe used media reports with some frequency. Individual teachers brought their own teaching style to bear on the general lesson structure shown in Chapter 4, page 77. The actions of Angela, Bob and Chloe are outlined below, quoting from their typical introductions to the activity, as these show some of their pedagogical approach.

Angela was the teacher with the most initial experience of using media reports in science lessons and was confident in using such materials. She was happy to adapt the materials and lesson outlines.

Angela introduced the report shown in Box 6.1, page 112, in the 'metals' module (Chem2 in Table 6.1) thus:

> Angela: So what we're going to do today – we're going to practise evaluating . . . And then if you apply what we do today to the real coursework tomorrow, you should be able to get yourselves some really, really good evaluation marks . . . two things we're going to do. The first we're going to do is to look at an experiment that some scientists have been doing . . . so we're going to look at the *New Scientist* article about their experiment and we're going to look at it to see what you think of it – how you evaluate their experiment. So in a way we're going to be criticizing their experiment to see if they have done it in a good way.

Typically for Angela, an introduction like this was followed by:

- students reading the article in silence;
- whole-class question and answer to ensure understanding of terminology that students have identified as difficult;
- students working individually, but able to communicate with their neighbour, on the questions posed;
- whole-class question and answer to discuss responses of students.

Part of Angela's summary of responses shows how typically she deals with each of the written questions for students in a purposeful and directive way:

> Angela: (about Question 3 – Is this evidence sufficient to support their claims?) . . . Can they be sure? – is a bit more tricky. Has anyone got something to read out to us about can they be sure?

Student: You don't know.

Angela: OK, why do you think you don't know?

Student: Not enough information about how many times they've done it.

Angela: OK, good – so there's some more things that you would like to know. So if I said, well, I actually know the person who did this experiment – what would you like me to ask them? Tell me some questions.

Student: How many times they'd done it.

Angela: OK. How many times they'd done it. I said to somebody but they could have tried it two thousand times – they could have tried it loads and loads of times over a large period of time. They've only summarized their findings there – so, yeh, we don't know how many times they did it. What else?

Student: How many times it's been successful.

Angela: OK. So we don't know the actual results – there's no results table there – so we're missing the actual results. This is just the conclusion – it doesn't show you the results table. Anything else it doesn't show you?

Student: Would it work on a larger scale?

It seemed easier for Angela to focus on (her and students') expectations of recording and reporting results rather than other aspects of research conduct. The provenance of the research and peer review in establishing validity of evidence were not explored.

Bob recognized his teaching style as very different from Angela's. Where Angela was very structured and somewhat repetitive in her instructions and comments, Bob was more informal. He had a willingness and confidence to try new approaches but not always the consistency to maintain developments. Bob's introduction in the same 'metals' module (Chem2) shows how his focus is on the article and its method of presentation:

Bob: These are written for the general scientific community, so scientists who want to know what's happening in the science world will buy a scientific journal. The same as Paul here will buy the *Beano*, to see what's happening in cartoon land (student laughter). These things are basically to give you a better general knowledge about science and the way science is carried out in the real world – not just a matter of like today we're going to do an experiment (in monotone) – write the title, set fire to something, have a laugh, mess about, write it up, did you learn anything? It's not done like that in the real world. So with the article first of all we're going to read through it as a class. The language is not meant for people your age. Some of you will find it easy to understand, some of you will find it hard. That's one of the things we'll discuss about it. So this one is to do with the topic we're on – metals.

Bob then went on to discuss the difference between this method of reporting and that in textbooks, highlighting the certainty of knowledge presented in textbooks and their lack of emphasis on how science is conducted.

For Bob, this introduction was followed by:

- different students reading the article out to the rest of the class;
- whole-class discussion of the article in general – its purpose and findings;
- extensive small group discussion of the questions with one scribe in each group recording answers;
- whole-class question and answer about the terminology used in the article and groups' responses to the questions.

Part of Bob's discussion of group responses shows how he deals with each question in turn, focusing mainly on some of the presentation issues:

Bob: Right. Let's go to the questions – number 1.
Student volunteers answer (inaudible)
Bob: OK, they claim they've found a way for bones to mend faster. Anything else? (pause)
Student: And they've mended a rabbit bone.
Bob: They claim that it works for rabbits.
Student: For the shin.
Bob: They claim that they found a way to mend bones faster and it works for rabbit bones – specially for shin bones.
Student: (inaudible)
Bob: OK, the second claim is they've found a way of doing this with titanium and apatite. What don't they claim, which is important?
Student: (inaudible)
Bob: Yeh, they don't claim that using titanium is their idea. Using apatite and titanium is not their idea – they said there – other researchers came up with this idea but, they're showing off, we found a way for it to work. So he's claiming that he got it to work, he's not claiming it's his idea. That's fine. Anything else?

It is notable that in both Angela's and Bob's discussion with students there are leading questions. They each anticipate taking the responses in a particular direction. The focus is on understanding the nature, recording and reporting of evidence, with Bob showing perhaps a wider perspective.

Chloe was keen to use media reports but initially found it difficult to structure the lesson. Chloe's introduction in 'humans as organisms' (Bio2), a different report, shows her sequencing of the task, again with a focus on conceptual understanding:

Chloe: We've been talking so far about organs in our module – started off the module talking about organs and we've gone through and talked about them individually. Last lesson we talked about lungs and we're going to go on to talk about the heart in tomorrow's lesson. So what we're going to do today is going to lead us nicely to it – be a bit of extra information for you. And it's all to do with the heart and cholesterol and diseases of the heart. *New Scientist* is like a big magazine, basically. Aimed at adults and yourselves as well, who should be interested in science. And what it is, is all the scientific research papers in the world are condensed down to make them easier reading so that we can understand them. 'Cos a lot of the actual main research journals are very wordy and long. And this is a much nicer way to present the information anyway. So this one . . . it's recently out of the press. But the idea today is to see how easily we can understand what's going on and how well we think this evidence was collected.

For Chloe, this introduction was followed by:

- different students reading the article out to the rest of the class, pausing to discuss words students had difficulty in understanding;
- students working individually, but able to communicate with their neighbour, on the questions posed.

No further time was available that lesson for whole-class discussion.

None of these regular users of media reports actually used reports in every module, as can be seen in Table 6.1. Lack of time was always the reason given. In using media reports, Angela's emphasis was on evaluating the work done by the scientists in relation to students' own investigations. Bob emphasized the nature of scientific research and the presentation issues in media reports. Chloe was keen to show the topicality and relevance to the science content under study. None of these approaches is wrong or right. They illustrate the way different teachers take the same material and put a particular emphasis on it according to their pedagogical goals and the way they view science. It would be very interesting to compare the approach an English or humanities teacher would take when considering the same media reports of science. They are more likely to focus on the presentational aspects, for example detecting bias, persuasion, genre, rather than on the nature of scientific endeavour portrayed.

Many of the teaching characteristics of the individual teachers are supported and, to some extent, explained by their responses to interview questions about their planning approaches and attitudes to curriculum change. Interview data allowed the identification of features that affect the way in which Angela, Bob, Chloe and Eric approach their week by week teaching. In summarizing the influences on lesson planning and implementation, we use a structure suggested by Lantz and Kass (1987). Empirical work led Lantz and Kass to consider that the following factors influence teachers' beliefs and values about science teaching and learning in their school setting (teachers' functional paradigm): policy documents and resulting curriculum materials; teachers' background – that is their own science education and teaching experience; the teaching situation – that is the nature of department and school. Lantz and Kass suppose that the paradigm, in turn, has a considerable effect on classroom practice. To this we add, as a summary from interview data, these teachers' views of how they consider that they would adjust their practice when faced with a voluntary and, then, a forced innovation (Figure 6.1). We offer cameos of these four teachers as they address a change in practice to incorporate media reports of science.

Angela had been teaching for eight years in a total of four different schools. She saw the departmental schemes of work and library of resources she had built up as big influences on her planning. As Head of Department she felt expectations on her for: keeping up to date with curriculum developments; observing and mentoring staff; and having overall responsibility for departmental schemes of work. In her teaching, Angela felt she was trying to satisfy competing demands – those of aiming for high exam results and satisfying parental concerns at the same time as motivating and interesting students in science and fulfilling her own interests as a teacher. These features led to preferred classroom practice of developing a balance of different activities across a week, the inclusion of a particular activity being based on informal evaluation of a previous occasion of using the activity. As a willing innovator, Angela saw interest in, and review of, new curriculum materials as a stimulus for change. She saw observation of other teachers' lessons and evaluations of curriculum materials as a source of support for change. In implementing the media report lessons, Angela saw the encouraging features as bringing up-to-date science into the classroom and increasing the literacy skills of the students. She felt preparation time and the risk in trying a new activity were discouraging factors: 'Having to take a risk, because realistically you don't really know what you're doing . . . And you're going to have some failures. You're going to do some things wrong with it.' If faced with an imposed innovation, Angela would develop a new scheme of work using expertise within the department or embedded in curriculum materials.

Bob had been teaching for five years in two different schools. Like Angela, he used the departmental scheme of work in his planning, but only in terms of providing expectations of the topic. His approach to teaching was far less structured than Angela. In describing the way he taught science Bob recognizes his informality: 'Oh, top of my head – and they never know what's coming and I don't do learning objectives because I think that ruins what's happening in the lesson, 'cos it's supposed to be suspense and 'I wonder what's going to

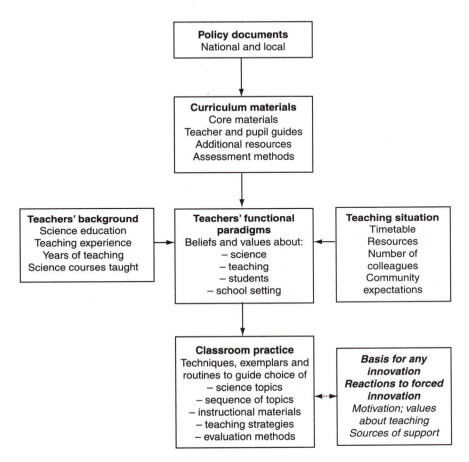

Figure 6.1   Model of teacher interpretation of curriculum materials (after Lantz and Kass 1987 – our addition in italics)

happen next.' He saw the school's expectations as him controlling learning, making it interesting and challenging. For Bob the main features influencing classroom practice were marrying the learning expectations of the scheme of work with keeping students motivated and learning. Bob was prepared to innovate. He was prepared to try anything, mostly using his own ideas but also assimilating others. Bob was surprised by his first trial of using a media report:

> I didn't think that would go down well when I first viewed it, but that lesson went really well. They had all sensible answers and they took it seriously . . . It's not the new material, it's not the articles and it wasn't the questions – it was just making it everyday life, making it realistic.

Like Angela he saw relevance as an important aspect, being less convinced about other possible outcomes from using up-to-date reports:

> The specific purpose of those things for improving kids' evaluation skills (pause) I don't know, I don't know about the importance of that. Well, I do know about the importance of it but I don't know how much time to give to evaluations when there's other things going on.

In contrast to Angela's acceptance of an imposed innovation, Bob felt he would only fully implement change if it were going to be formally examined or fitted with his existing teaching approach.

Chloe had less teaching experience than Angela and Bob, but in her three years of teaching had still taught in two schools. As with Angela and Bob, the scheme of work was a starting point in her planning. Chloe saw the school's expectations as her delivering the curriculum in a way that fully involved the students. She saw herself stressing the applications of science, using models and striving for perfection in promoting student enjoyment and full understanding. She wished to be creative and was thus open to innovation. She saw this as affecting her planning:

> I'd see the materials first and if they looked interesting I'd try slotting them into the scheme of work . . . If I've got something to teach that I think looks really boring . . . then I'll really try to find a way of teaching it that turns it right round and even if you can't teach it through an application I'd try and do it in a fun way – role-play or cartoons.

Although Chloe was willing to innovate she felt in need of support in using new materials and approaches in her lessons, seeking advice from colleagues and, in particular, the researcher (the first author).

Each of these teachers showed willingness to innovate but uncertainty in practice in stepping outside the norms of science teaching in opening up issues for discussion. Eric is included here as an example of someone who seemed reluctant to engage in the project from the outset. With a degree in physics, he had five years' teaching experience in three schools. Like the other teachers, the scheme of work was a starting point in his planning, using it as a guide but reacting to students' understanding from one lesson to the next. He saw the school's expectations on him as teaching for high exam grades, with student enjoyment being secondary. Eric felt the concepts of science were important:

> I would like them to be able to leave after a year of science with me, a school lifetime of science with me, or whatever, knowing that an understanding of science was useful and having some explanation of everyday phenomena and being able to explain it and being able to go

in the pub at 18 and say 'Well, you know why that's got hot don't you, bla bla', and just waffle on about it and be able to drop science into the conversation.

Eric needed convincing that an innovation would be beneficial. He was the only one of the four who required external evidence of the efficacy of change in order to start to modify his practice:

> The other thing is evidence of success I suppose – or evidence of failure but they don't often arrive with that – evidence of success, where you've seen or heard people talking about it, in a similar situation to your own – rather than saying, Oh, it's wonderful – in this fantastic, single-sex private school.

In addition, he admitted he would be likely to pay lip-service to an innovation on the grounds of reluctance to change, or attempt to argue that the innovation was already in operation in his classroom. Eric would be willing to try changing practice:

> Um, I'd like to think I'd always do it a second time – just on the basis that if you do anything once you're not going to be very good at it yourself. Um, and equally, if you're not very good at it and/or a different class will take to it differently. So, ideally I'd go for it twice I suppose. If it didn't work on either of these occasions I'd probably be binning it.

As with Chloe, the researcher worked with Eric in using media reports in one lesson. However, despite his professed willingness, he did not try activities further. He was not convinced of the benefits of using media reports based on this experience.

Angela, Bob and Chloe considered that only internal support is necessary for implementing curriculum change, while Eric would seek external evidence of the success of any innovation. Across the four teachers, the impression is that they have the confidence and ability to promote student learning of *science* without additional support, adapting their teaching according to their previous experience of using a particular activity. They see implementation of change as being based on their own experience, with outside support being mainly in the form of useful resources. It appears with these teachers that only if the materials have some coincidence with teachers' interests and goals are there real attempts at incorporation into lessons, despite the support and encouragement offered. In this, Angela was the most successful and persistent, possibly because she had more ownership from the outset. Chloe's professed interest in the materials and the idea of curriculum change did not in itself overcome the barrier to full implementation with a mixed-ability class. She asked the researcher to help her lead the activities in order to assist with teaching strategies. This procedure encouraged her to adapt the last media report for inclusion in the Environment module for which she had responsibility. Chloe took ownership at this stage and has continued to use media reports in different ways. Joyce and Showers (1995) argue that full implementation of a curriculum change with externally set goals requires mediation and support by people with full understanding and expertise in reaching such goals. Bob and Eric might be seen as subversive to any imposed change: in Bob's case due to his ad hoc approach to planning and with Eric his self-identified resistance to change.

It is interesting to note the responses of the whole department to the project when planning for the next year of the course. All were positive about the impact of the involvement, despite the lack of uptake by two of the department present – Don and Fran. (Eric excused himself from the departmental discussion due to pressure of other work.) All the teachers made claims for improved learning and motivation even though in some cases there had been little apparent uptake of suggested approaches. Witness this exchange between Don (who appeared to have tried one only media report lesson as planned) and Angela:

> Don: I would say that using the articles purely and simply to hone their evaluation skills has actually been productive with my kids in that, although they've had difficulty accessing the language because they're not bright kids, they are stimulated to discuss the articles, they're actually engaged by the articles. They're interested in them and they have developed their ability to evaluate information they're given.
>
> Angela: I agree that it's extended their criticism of things. I don't think they stop to think too often of 'well, is that the best way?' I think maybe probably we haven't been trained up each year teaching evaluation skills, that all of a sudden we've started teaching evaluation skills – whereas we might not have done that teaching in the past.

Despite this exchange, we feel an important value teachers placed on the activities was the opportunity to bring current scientific research into lessons rather than focus on the processes of science. This may be explained by how they saw the focus of the curriculum and its assessment system, as Bob indicates:

> In science the only thing they get credit for when they leave here after five years of teaching them is their knowledge and what they can reproduce and their ability to copy out of the textbook a bit of scientific theory to back up an investigation they've done. Yes, you can

teach them all about what it is to be a scientist and stuff but what they get evaluated on is recall, and some understanding I suppose.

However, the impact of introducing media reports may bring less tangible changes than those observed during the particular lessons. As Angela indicates,

I think that I've probably taught evaluation skills better this year because of thinking about it. They've been more interested in it because of this and I'm getting higher marks for evaluations than before, with lower ability kids.

In a later part we will look at the validity of these claims in examining students' reactions to this innovation.

Implications for teacher development

It seems that attitudes towards innovation are laid down early on in teaching experience – both Chloe and Eric highlighted particular successful experiences in their postgraduate training year but with different reactions to innovation based on this. Although all of the teachers interviewed had worked in more than one school, and thus may be adaptable, they could all be considered as in the early stages of their teaching career. Flexibility and approaches to curriculum change need to be considered from the outset in teacher training. Allowing teachers to articulate explicitly their beliefs about teaching (functional paradigms), and evaluating them alongside the goals of particular curriculum materials, may encourage more considered evaluation of curriculum innovation.

The outcomes of this case study have both positive and negative features as regards teacher change for science education for citizenship. Positively as:

- Teachers saw the inclusion of media reports in a scheme of work as a benefit to student learning and they have continued the collection and development of media-based activities.
- Two teachers persisted with the activities as intended during the year with continued or improved levels of performance in student evaluation of evidence (see next section).

Negatively as:

- Only one-third of intended reports were used. Penetration of the implemented curriculum was low, time and teacher attitude being major factors.

- The intended emphasis on the processes of scientific research and evaluation of evidence seemed to be modified for most teachers more towards a focus on the up-to-date content of the scientific research and its links with the science topic being studied.

Student learning about the nature of scientific endeavour

Part of the motivation for this action research in examining student learning was in extending evidence from other studies. One aim we might have in exploring socio-scientific issues is assisting students to understand the links between accumulation of scientific evidence and generation of theory. The relationship between the two is not straightforward but is important in helping students to understand the nature of scientific endeavour (see Table 1.1, page 19).

Several researchers have explored people's understanding of the nature of scientific research, including attempts to clarify the nature and development of students' reasoning in considering the relationship between evidence and theory. These have usually been done in settings outside the classroom – using group interviews (Driver *et al*. 1996); responses to problems requiring reasoning (Kuhn *et al*. 1988); or questionnaires (Norris and Phillips 1994; Solomon *et al*. 1996). These studies suggest that students' abilities are developmental, but context-dependency may account for their different findings. For example, Kuhn *et al* (1988), from examining the reasoning of different age groups, argue that skills of distinguishing between evidence and theory are underdeveloped even in adults. Samarapungavan (1992), however, shows that even young children are 'capable of coordinating theories with evidence and reasoning rationally in both theory selection and theory production contexts'. Findings from such research give little guidance as to what might be achieved in supportive classrooms or how to tackle the teaching of 'evidence and theory' – hence this attempt to explore students' capabilities in a learning context.

We restate here the intended learning outcomes for these media report activities in focusing on student learning (see also Chapter 4, page 65). Most of these are concerned with conceptual knowledge.

We wished students to be able to:

- distinguish between results and conclusions;
- identify levels of certainty in drawing conclusions;
- understand how to *draw a conclusion consistent with the evidence and relate this to scientific knowledge and understanding* (procedural knowledge);
- *comment on the reliability of the evidence, accounting for any anomalous*

results or explain whether the evidence is sufficient to support a firm conclusion;
- *propose improvements, or further work, to provide additional evidence for the conclusion, or to extend the enquiry.*

(Those items in italics refer to assessed aspects of students' scientific investigations.)

To exemplify the student responses, we will concentrate on two reports, which were used with the greatest frequency. The report entitled 'Bouncing back' (Box 6.1) was used in the unit on metals, whose main focus was the reactivity series and the use of metals. The report on traffic research (Box 6.3) was used in an environment unit which all classes did at the end of the year. Angela's, Bob's and Chloe's classes used the report. In addition, a 'control' class at another school doing the same GCSE course answered the questions during a science lesson, but without any prior teaching or intervention by the teacher.

The lessons were audio-taped and students' written work collected. In addition, field notes recorded the key activities. Some student discussion was captured but written work was principally used to explore students' reasoning. We regard the written work as showing the *minimum* level of reasoning that students might be using in the context of a teacher-supported activity as students did not always record all their thinking or discussion.

In order to make comparisons between students' responses to different reports we categorized students' reasoning in the following way:

- Mature reasoning: claim of researchers identified fully or partially; evidence for claim identified fully or partially; recognition of insufficient evidence; suggestions made for further work.
- Partial reasoning: claim of researchers identified fully or partially; evidence for claim identified fully or partially; recognition of insufficient evidence with no suggestions for further work or evidence is regarded as sufficient but suggestions are made for further work.
- Naïve reasoning: claim of researchers identified fully or partially; evidence for claim identified fully or partially; evidence sufficient; no suggestions for further work.
- Incomplete response: claim of researchers identified fully or partially or evidence for claim identified fully or partially.

Mature reasoning is classified as such because the claims in reports are presented with some caveats – for example, the researchers comment on the limitations of their methodology or evidence, or other researchers express some scepticism. Examples of these responses are shown for the two reports (see Boxes 6.2 and 6.4).

Box 6.1 Text of a report from *New Scientist* on research into materials 31 January 1998

Bouncing back
Coated titanium is mending broken bones fast

AN INJURED Japanese rabbit was quickly back on its feet again thanks to a breakthrough in rapid bone-mending techniques. The animal's fractured tibia, or shin bone, mended quickly when small slivers of coated titanium were inserted into the break.

Researchers from Kyoto University, who carried out the experiment, say that the new material not only heals fractures faster but is stronger than other methods of mending bones, including allowing the bone to heal naturally – the approach preferred by most British surgeons.

Researchers have long known that, in theory at least, pieces of metal could act as an anchor to help synostosis – the process by which new bone grows and joins together after a fracture.

In practice, however, it has proved difficult to find a suitable material for the anchor. Titanium is a good candidate because it is light, tough and non-corrosive. But bone does not graft to it.

Apatite, a naturally occurring mineral of calcium phosphate, has almost the opposite properties to titanium. Bone readily grows around it, but it is too fragile to be used in load-bearing bones. Previous attempts to combine the two materials have not been successful.

The researchers at Kyoto say that their new method gives the pieces of titanium an almost seamless coating that contains a mixture of apatite and titanium oxide. This allows bone to graft to the outside of the coating while the inner core remains strong and durable.

The finishing process involves heating pieces of titanium in an alkaline solution to a temperature of 600°C and then depositing the coating. The coating gradates from 100 per cent titanium oxide on the inside, which binds strongly with the titanium, to 100 per cent apatite on the outside, which binds to the new bone that grows naturally to mend the fracture.

'The graded structure is very important,' says Tadashi Kokubo of Kyoto University's material chemistry department. He says that although other researchers have come up with the idea of combining apatite and titanium to make a strong anchor for bone growth before, they had not succeeded in making the apatite stick to the metal. 'Previous methods of coating titanium with apatite involved plasma spraying at over 1000°C. But the powder decomposed and wouldn't bind tightly.'

Kokubo says his tests with small pieces of titanium 1 centimetre square and 1 millimetre thick have been so successful that he is moving on to healing fractures in larger sheep bones, using coated titanium screws. After that he wants to go on and perform trials on human patients.

Peter Hadfield, Tokyo

Box 6.2   Examples of students' reasoning about 'Bouncing back'

Mature reasoning

Q1 Found a new way of repairing broken bones in rabbits by using titanium and apatite. He also claims he's found a way of joining titanium and apatite which has not been done before. Claims best method.

Q2 The evidence to support his research is small. It does show the researcher's way of mending the bone but this has only occurred on one rabbit.

Q3 Solid proof would be getting the same results a number of times. The results also have no proof it will work on other animals and humans. This evidence is not sufficient to say it will work every time.

Q4 Do tests again on rabbits, different types of breaks and different animals including humans. Try and find another metal.

Q5 The researchers have evidence that their [*sic*] the first methods of others attempts. Show their method and explain almost step by step. Shows their work.

Partial reasoning

Q1 The researchers claim they can make broken bones heal quicker using apatite coated titanium.

Q2 It says that they coat the titanium with apatite [*sic*] because it can graft to that but not to the titanium but the titanium is stronger and more durable and they have tested it on a rabbit and it worked.

Q3 Yes because titanium properties are very strong, light and durable.

Q4 Do it on a human bone to see if it works on humans and try out other metals.

Naïve reasoning

Q1 Because titanium mends the bones; heals them faster

Q2 Because the bone heals faster and they have done test

Q3 Yes I think they have prove there [*sic*] idea enough because they prove it works

Incomplete

Q1 The researchers are claiming that bones can be fixed using metal

Q2 The researchers know that their ideas work because they have experimented on the rabbit.

Those students showing 'mature reasoning' showed recognition of the type of evidence being presented and its limitations. The example of mature reasoning for 'traffic calming' in Box 6.4 is unusual in that there is a comment on the model underpinning the research. It was very rare for students to comment on links between evidence and theory in this way. As we felt it important to use authentic reports whose content linked with the topic under study we did not adapt the reports to make them similar in

---

Box 6.3   Text of a report from *New Scientist* on research into pollution
13 January 1999

How calmer traffic stays green

FEARS that road humps can increase pollution are unfounded, according to a new study in Britain.

Road humps are very effective at slowing traffic in residential streets, and this can cut serious accidents by as much as a third. But motoring organisations have claimed that such 'traffic calming' could increase emissions of pollutants such as nitrogen dioxide by a factor of 10 because these emissions increase when cars travel slowly. This has been used as an argument against humps, says Derek Palmer of the London-based Institution of Highways and Transportation.

Now the Transport Research Laboratory in Crowthorne, Berkshire, has shown that introducing a traffic-calming scheme does not necessarily increase pollution. The TRL asked 20 people to drive a car on selected routes in Havant, Hampshire, both before and after humps were introduced. 'We wanted something that was representative of the way people really drive,' says Jane Cloke, one of the team.

The speed of the car was recorded on these journeys, and this information was fed into a computer model that predicts the emissions of different pollutants from various types of car. The researchers also monitored traffic patterns in the area before and after humps were introduced. Taken together, these measurements showed there was a slight drop in emissions both inside and outside the traffic-calming area, although Cloke says 'it didn't make a huge amount of difference'.

The chief reason for this finding, says Cloke, is that drivers using residential roads as a short cut had to stop and start at the numerous junctions along the route. When the introduction of humps forced these drivers onto main roads, the smoother traffic flow cut the cars' emissions. The TRL plans to publish its results in detail later this year.

Mick Hamer

---

complexity. Students seemed to find it easier to discuss 'bouncing back' than 'traffic calming' with its more complex research comparison. Despite the lack of uniformity in reports, we made some overall comparisons of reasoning across the year. Table 6.2 shows the reasoning levels for the classes on these two reports only (for simplicity) and the total across all reports used. Most students were able to answer questions in their own words, showing some understanding of the thrust of the report. Few students showed naïve reasoning, with many able to argue for the type of work which could be done to extend the research presented. Suggestions for further work varied from a general exhortation for more testing (six per cent of the 191 suggestions) to consideration of a range of different variables to alter. Many students made more than one suggestion, the largest proportion (53 per cent) arguing for

---

Box 6.4   Examples of students' reasoning about 'Traffic Calming'

Mature reasoning
Q1 Speed bumps force people onto main roads less start and stop – less emission
Q2 TRL did tests on 20 cars – measured speeds and calculated emissions using a computer model
Q3 Model might not be accurate. More than 20.
Q4 More than 20. Measure actual emissions. Different cars.

Partial reasoning
Q1 That nitrogen dioxide from car emissions is released more when the car is travelling slowly
That the road humps don't make much difference from cars giving out more pollution.
Q2 They got people to drive 20 cars in Havant where there are traffic calming conditions like humps and measured the speed of the cars and then could see how much pollution was given off.
Q3 It is quite sufficient but they could of [*sic*] been tested in different conditions e.g. different weather, age of car
Q4 It could have been tested in different conditions e.g. different weather, age of car

Naïve reasoning
Q1 They claim that humps don't make much difference
Q2 When cars drive fast emissions increase but not by much
Q3 Yes

Incomplete
Q1 'When car is travelling slowly increase of emissions of nitrogen dioxide' This is wrong. There was not a lot of difference.
Q2
Q3 Yes because they did a fair test and found their [*sic*] wasn't a lot of people.

---

repeating the research for different named variables. Other suggestions, which were report dependent, included a larger sample size (17 per cent) or a larger scale or longer time (17 per cent). Three per cent suggested repeating the research as given.

Statistical comparison, using t-tests, between each class on all reports suggests that the reasoning of those who were initially operating at a low level did improve with increased exposure to the reports and structured questions. Certainly, the students in the control class did not show as high a level of reasoning as students who had experienced some use of media reports throughout the year.

Table 6.2 Responses to two particular media reports from each class

Class	Report	N	Reasoning			
			Mature	*Partial*	*Naïve*	*Incomplete*
Angela	Metals	16	8	3	1	5
Angela	Traffic	12	6	4	1	1
Bob	Metals	17	5	6	1	4
Bob	Traffic	6	5	0	1	0
Chloe	Metals	15	13	0	0	2
Chloe	Traffic	11	10	0	0	1
Eric	Metals	19	12	3	4	0
Total Metals		67	38 (57%)	12 (18%)	6 (9%)	11 (16%)
Total Traffic		29	21 (72%)	4 (14%)	2 (7%)	2 (7%)
Total for all reports used in the school		188	89 (47%)	35 (19%)	15 (8%)	49 (26%)
Control class	Traffic	22	6 (27%)	7 (32%)	5 (23%)	4 (18%)

Given that the students covered the full achievement range, what can be said about students' learning from this experience? The results may suggest what we might realistically expect of students in a supported situation. At one level the student responses are optimistic. A significant proportion of all classes could show mature reasoning but progression and reinforcement may depend on the opportunities given within the classroom to develop evaluation skills systematically. At the outset of this intervention we did not know what reaction we would get from the students – would the reports be perceived as difficult and irrelevant or would they promote discussion? Although the activities were not that memorable, as indicated from student interview data at the end of the year, responses to Bob's spontaneous question to his class in one lesson surprised him. Having discussed the report on broken bones, he asked the class whether they would prefer to learn from a textbook or from reports such as this. Overwhelmingly, the students responded enthusiastically to the opportunity to discuss the media report. They argued that the science presented in textbooks was boring, factual and did not give a feel for what scientists really did.

As free-standing activities, students enjoyed reading and could analyse authentic reports of science research. However, the aims of assisting evaluations of students' own investigations and their understanding of the *principles* of sound scientific research did not appear to be fully realized. There was low correlation between individual students' reasoning about the media reports and their achievements in evaluating their own investigations or their overall performance in investigations, according to assessment criteria (that is in contradiction to Don and Angela's claims). We felt that students had reasoned in the context of particular media reports but that reinforcement was needed.

A particular limitation of this study in supporting and exploring student learning is the nature of the questions posed to students. In retrospect, the particular questions were perhaps not the best for exploring the nature of scientific endeavour. (More appropriate questions are indicated in Chapter 4, page 77.) However, teachers considered that the need to integrate the activity with a key part of the science curriculum – in this case students' own investigations – was paramount in encouraging uptake of the activities. As can be seen, even with this integration there was not extensive use by all teachers. If we consider that recognition of elements of scientific research is important in allowing citizens to develop informed views on scientific controversies and advancements, then systematic development of skills during compulsory education is necessary.

7 Decision-making about socio-scientific issues

The two case studies in this chapter focus on students' use of a framework in promoting their procedural understanding of decision-making. In addition we explore the constructs, science and values they used in their discussions. The second case study examines the role of the teacher in chairing and supporting decision-making discussions.

Decision-making as a process

Decision-making implies commitment to a choice made voluntarily and from which deliberate action follows. For the purposes of the research we undertook, it was acknowledged that the socio-scientific issues under consideration represent real problems, but are not always ones in which students will either want or be able to demonstrate commitment to the decision made. Most of the tasks carried out by students are ones in which they developed 'informed opinions'. The difference between an 'informed opinion' and an 'informed decision' is subtle but important. Opinion forming implies that commitment is not necessarily present (attitude formation) whereas decision-making implies finality and action (behaviour). Decision-making in our research is concerned with developing informed opinions. However, decision-making as a term will continue to be used because it is adopted so extensively throughout the literature to describe tasks and research of a similar nature.

Making decisions about biological conservation

Our first case study looks at groups of 15- to 16-year-olds as they used the decision-making framework shown in Chapter 4 (page 80) in unsupported peer group discussions. We wanted to gain an insight into how they interacted with each other and how they used biological concepts and identified value positions, and to see whether peer group decision-making exercises affected their views towards biological conservation.

Conservation of the world's diversity of organisms and genetic resources (biological conservation) is an emotive socio-scientific issue which inevitably affects, and is affected by, human social and economic development. Biological conservation can be regarded as a precondition for sustainable development. Numerous and varied figures abound about the number of species being lost to extinction as a result of human activity (UNEP 1995).

Biological conservation involves making tough decisions about what and how to conserve – because we are obviously not going to save everything! Successful conservation management programmes rely on an understanding of the biology of the organisms concerned and, as with all socio-scientific issues, economics, politics and cultural aspects also play an important role in this decision-making process. Professional conservation biologists have identified a large number of biological concepts as essential underpinnings for school education programmes (Grace and Ratcliffe 2002). However, there are theorists who criticize the scientific orientation of conservation management (Yearly 1991; Harrison 1993), and some believe that cultural, aesthetic or utilitarian factors are equally, if not more, important in deciding conservation priorities (Spellerberg 1996).

Despite its importance among biologists, and considerable media coverage, young people still fail to consider biological conservation as a high priority environmental issue (Stanisstreet *et al.* 1993). A survey of over a thousand 15- and 16-year-olds revealed that just 34 per cent regarded the loss of animal and plant species as a 'very serious' issue, and they ranked it lower than ozone layer depletion, destruction of tropical rainforest, global warming and the greenhouse effect (Morris and Schagen 1996).

Implementation of the decision-making framework

Decision-making tasks were used with 131 15-year-old students (61 girls and 70 boys), at four different coeducational schools in the south of England. All were above average achievers in science. The students were divided into 24 'peer groups' (four to six per group) which were small groups of their own choice – some single-sexed and some mixed. They were asked to consider specific conservation scenarios using the decision-making framework, and think about any factors they thought important in making these decisions, but, as it was a science lesson, to focus particularly on the scientific information needed. The researcher (the second author) did not intervene in discussions other than managing procedural aspects of the activity, and no teachers or classroom assistants were involved during this time. Student discussions were audio-taped and analysed for: use of scientific concepts; inclusion of value positions taken; the nature of peer interactions within the groups. The groups were also asked to produce a written account of their progress at each stage of the decision-making framework.

The tasks related to one of two real conservation scenarios, one concerning the conservation of elephants in Africa, the other the conservation of puffins (a well-known British seabird) in competition with rabbits. Elephants, puffins and rabbits were chosen for the study as species that these students would have a relatively strong desire to conserve. Studies have shown that 'intelligent' and 'beautiful' animals receive the most positive attitudes among young people (Greaves *et al.* 1993; Grace and Sharp 2000b). Elephants, puffins and rabbits fall into these categories. Both issues were introduced by way of very brief written information and accompanying colour photographs of the animals involved. The scenarios were similar in that elephants and puffins are endangered species. However, elephant conservation is very much more of a social issue, having considerable impact potentially on local economies through tourism, crop destruction and the ivory trade. The puffin conservation scenario, on the other hand, is presented as a less complex issue where there is no significant impact on the local human population. Puffins are seabirds which nest in burrows in the soil on cliffs and islands around the coast of Britain. Expanding rabbit populations cause soil erosion and compete for space. Both scenarios can be regarded as one step removed from students' immediate experience – that is, they are not personal or local issues.

The nature of the dialogue in unsupported peer group discussions

We discuss three features from the discussions:

- the impact on students' views and the nature of peer interaction;
- the use of biological concepts underpinning conservation;
- the use of values and integration with scientific knowledge.

Students' views and peer interaction

We first explore the attitudes and views of students towards the particular conservation issues. To evaluate any changes, students were asked prior to the activity, and under test conditions, to write their own views on how to tackle the conservation issues. This was repeated immediately after the discussion. For both scenarios, students provided a range of solutions, and a comparison of individual choices at the pre- and post- stages may indicate the possible impact of the group discussion on their views. A fundamental choice affecting the final decision was whether some animals should be killed (or culled) in order to protect others. This aspect accounted for a substantial part of the conversation in all discussion groups.

Most youngsters at this age view species extinction as an unacceptable consequence of human activities (Grace and Sharp 2000b). However, girls are known to be more environmentally aware and active than boys, tending to express a more 'sympathetic' view, and stronger positive attitude towards conservation (Morris and Schagen 1996). It might seem to follow that girls are less favourably disposed towards the killing (culling) of individual animals. Table 7.1 shows that before and after the discussion, more boys than girls chose culling elephants and rabbits, and although more people advocated culling rabbits than elephants, the gender difference was fairly consistent for both scenarios. After the discussion, there was a marked increase in advocating culling among both boys and girls.

The majority of students initially chose another solution which did not involve culling (e.g. constructing fences, relocating or sterilizing animals). However, after discussion many of these changed their views or elected for a combination of ideas as a solution to the problem. The minority who held the same view before and after are shown in Table 7.2. This shows that slightly more girls than boys gave a consistent response.

As a result of the discussions, therefore, over 70 per cent of students modified their solutions to the conservation issues in some way. This change in attitude supports Solomon's (1992b) suggestion that group discussion can assist attitude change. It contrasts, however, with Aikenhead's (1991) hypothesis that, in resolving conceptual conflicts, group decisions emerge from members' original choice preferences, rather than from their interactions

Table 7.1 Percentage of girls and boys advocating culling as a conservation management solution

	Pre-test attitude			Post-test attitude		
	% of girls (n = 61)	% of boys (n = 70)	% of all pupils (n = 131)	% of girls (n = 61)	% of boys (n = 70)	% of all pupils (n = 131)
Cull rabbits	16	25	21	28	36	32
Cull elephants	12	17	15	20	26	23

Table 7.2 Percentage of students who remained consistent over their choices

	% of girls (n = 61)	% of boys (n = 70)	% of all pupils (n = 131)
Puffin scenario	27	21	24
Elephant scenario	29	26	27

during discussion. In the present study the peer group friendship seemed sufficiently robust to allow disagreement without much personal conflict. There were signs that discussion of conservation issues reduced the rigidity of views and brought students towards a compromise view. This is noticeable, for example, when considering gender differences. As a result of the discussions, girls appear to become more favourably disposed towards culling, and boys become more prepared to investigate alternative options to culling.

The students remained fully engaged when discussing these conservation issues. Very few groups stuck rigidly to the framework, but used it as an aid to keeping on task. To provide a more detailed picture of peer interaction we examine the key features of two particular discussions by the same peer group (two girls and two boys). One discussion is on elephants and one on puffins. There were some stereotypical male comments at the start of the discussions, recommending that the rabbits and elephants be shot for sport and human pleasure, but this tended to be brief. The initial view among the girls was to avoid killing rabbits and elephants. The initial view of one of the boys was to kill rabbits, but not elephants. The other boy was prepared to go either way as long as it was practical. The individual students did not necessarily make the same value judgements about culling elephants and rabbits. For example, one girl commented: 'elephants deserve more respect (than rabbits) because they are more intelligent'.

Despite the difference between the two scenarios, it was noticeable how each individual had a consistent approach in both discussions, even though their views on the two issues sometimes differed. For example, one boy played a fairly passive role throughout, generally agreeing with the others' opinions. Interestingly, this boy's private written decision after the activity differed from the decision that he had agreed to as part of the group. In this case there was a feeling that he had agreed with his peers for an easy life! However, he seemed to be unusual in this respect, and most students did show signs of modifying their personal decisions subsequent to the discussions. The other three students had very strong and opposing views about killing animals at the beginning of the discussion, but their final group decision was a compromise between the two view points perhaps moving towards an acceptable public consensus (Chapter 1, page 16). In these cases they decided to carry out a limited cull if no other options were feasible. Overall science played little part in the discussion, and their decision-making was based on a few key values.

The use of biological concepts in decision-making discussions
The decision-making discussions proved useful in helping ascertain which aspects of science content were drawn upon while considering the issues. During the decision-making activity, students were deliberately encouraged to clarify any relevant scientific information they had or required. Of the 45 biological concepts identified as essential by experts (Grace and Ratcliffe

2002), 20 concepts were used or mentioned by students in total; 18 while discussing the elephant issue and 15 while discussing puffins (Table 7.3). For a 40-minute discussion this may sound as if scientific concepts were used extensively to inform the discussion, but the only concepts raised and discussed by *all* groups in both scenarios were 'species', 'rarity' and 'culling'. In both scenarios, some terms were conceptualized, but not necessarily mentioned by name. The concept of 'habitat' was often implied by referral to the place where these animals lived. Conversely some concepts were mentioned by name, but not in the established scientific sense. For example, 'natural selection' was mentioned by four groups, but in the sense of letting nature take its course, despite human intervention, rather than letting evolution continue naturally.

Table 7.3 Concepts used by students during decision-making, in rank order of frequency

Concepts used by students	Elephants (12 groups)	Puffins (12 groups)	Total (24 groups)
Culling of animals*	12	12	24
Rarity*	12	12	24
Species*	12	12	24
Food chains*	10	11	21
Translocation of species	8	11	19
Habitats*	9	8	17
Animal behaviour	5	12	17
Populations*	7	7	14
Competition*	1	12	13
Extinction now*	8	0	8
Ecosystems*	4	4	8
Food webs*	4	2	6
Sexual reproduction	3	3	6
Animal physiology	4	1	5
Introduced species	0	1	1
Extinction in the past	0	1	1
Genetic mutation	1	0	1
Inheritance	1	0	1
Gene pools	1	0	1
Genes	1	0	1
Environmental pollution*	0	0	0
Natural selection*	0	0	0
Adaptation*	0	0	0
Natural population fluctuations*	0	0	0
Evolution in the past*	0	0	0
Total	18	15	20

(Asterisks indicate the concepts that over 50% of teachers expected pupils to consider)

Although the ultimate objective of biological conservation is to avoid extinction, the concept of 'extinction' featured in most (eight) elephant discussions, but was not considered in any puffin discussions. This reflects findings by Greaves *et al.* (1993) that when British children of this age were asked to list any animals that were endangered, elephants were the most frequently named (by 53 per cent of students), and the only British animals mentioned were foxes and badgers (which are not particularly endangered species anyway). It is evident from the discussion above that students are unlikely to draw on many of the important biological concepts let alone successfully integrate them in practical decision-making. It would be interesting to see how teachers also view the relevance of these concepts and their integration, and this aspect is examined more closely later in this section.

The use of values in decision-making discussions

Conservation biology is driven by the *value* of biodiversity, and environmental philosophers commonly divide values into two main types (Callicott 1997):

1 anthropocentric or utilitarian values, which are useful to humans in some way;
2 biocentric, intrinsic or ethical values, which are inherently valuable as ends in themselves.

As the peer group decision-making deliberations proceeded, more weight tended to be given to 'values' than to scientific concepts. The values used in the discussions (Table 7.4) indicate that ethics were a major consideration. Every group raised ethical issues in both scenarios, mostly in terms of animal rights. Anthropomorphism featured in some group discussions (four in each scenario). One group mused over the effect of sterilizing rabbits to control the population, with one student remarking: '. . . but they'll [the rabbits] get all annoyed if they can't breed!' This type of comment emphasizes the sometimes inextricable links between science concepts and values. Among utilitarian values, all groups discussed the animals in an aesthetic sense, using words such as 'friendly', 'cute' and 'pretty' to support arguments for conserving them. All but two of the groups discussed economic values such as the cost of electric fencing around farms in Africa, and the economics of finding and relocating rabbits or puffins. Other values, such as effectiveness, altruism and safety, were more context-dependent, being more frequently raised in association with the elephant issue, which directly involved human interests.

Teachers' expectations of use of science and values

We now consider how these peer group discussions compare with teachers' expectations of students' action. Thirty-four science teachers, from a variety of

Table 7.4 Frequency of values used by pupils during decision-making, compared with teacher expectations

Values	Elephants 12 groups	Puffins 12 groups	Percentage of teachers expecting these values (puffins only)
Biocentric (intrinsic/ethical)			
Right to live, 'You can't say a puffin has more right to live than a rabbit.'	12	12	85
Anthropomorphism 'But they'll [rabbits] get all annoyed if they can't breed!'	4	4	18
Anthropocentric (utilitarian)			
Aesthetic/enjoyment 'cute', 'pretty', 'friendly'	12	12	26
Economic/cost 'How much would it cost to find and move all of them?'	12	10	3
Effectiveness 'An electric fence won't necessarily stop a herd of elephants.'	10	4	11
Altruism/future generations 'The people need to eat even if it means killing some elephants.'	11	0	0
Safety 'Elephants can kill people when they're frightened.'	4	1	0
Information/scientific research	0	0	0

schools, were provided with the experts' list of essential biological concepts, and asked to rate how important these were for students to study in order to make decisions about biological conservation issues. Ten of these teachers were purposely sampled as the science teachers of the students who took part in the study; but there appeared to be no discernible difference in the responses of this group compared with the other 24. The teachers were also provided with the puffin conservation scenario and asked what values and scientific concepts they thought students would include while making decisions about the issue. Although on average the teachers rated all the biological concepts as important in underpinning conservation decision-making, they tended to rate 'ecological concepts' (such as food webs and habitats) more highly than 'genetics concepts'. Variation within species, for example, was rated as 'essential' by less than 13 per cent of the teachers. This is surprising since the importance of genetics to conservation issues has been well established for more than twenty years (IUCN 1980).

Not surprisingly, this ecology–genetics divide was also reflected in teachers' expectation of concepts that students would use when making decisions about the issues (indicated by asterisks in Table 7.3). If we look at the concepts raised more than once by students, teachers' predictions of the concepts used were fairly accurate (10 out of 14 concepts predicted). As predicted by teachers, most groups discussed 'ecological concepts', and it is noticeable how only one group discussed concepts relating to genetics and inheritance, perhaps reflecting teachers' relatively low rating of these concepts.

The inclusion of values considerations in conservation education is important and expected. Table 7.4 indicates that teachers were fairly accurate in their prediction of the values students would use. Thus it would appear that the science teachers knew their students well enough to predict the biological concepts, and even the values that they would draw on when making decisions about conservation issues. However, since the teachers themselves regarded some concepts as more important than others, these views will inevitably shape the way they teach conservation, and influence students' ability to draw on the necessary concepts in such a decision-making exercise. Biological conservation is often taught as a value-free scientific discipline, and this may impede learning. Brody (1994) found that scientific knowledge related to ecological crises does not increase with age, and suggests that this is because such issues are not associated with science concepts taught in the classroom. This emphasizes the need to integrate science with values when considering socio-scientific issues.

Summary of outcomes of unsupported peer group decision-making

Post-test questionnaires revealed that the great majority of students (87 per cent) found the task 'useful' or 'very useful' in assisting their development of informed opinions. Interviews also confirmed that students preferred to work on the issues in small groups rather than on their own. Students tended to remain on-task and stayed fully engaged in decision-making. Some students were initially very rigid in their views and exposure to and consideration of the views of others demonstrated the benefit of discussing the issues with peers. Students did not bring much science into the discussion, and it would appear that very specific prompting is needed for students to relate conservation issues to the underlying scientific principles. The discussions inevitably involved values as well as scientific evidence, and more weight was given to values as the discussions proceeded. There were also signs that their use of values and scientific concepts was context-dependent, indicating a need for them to discuss a range of conservation scenarios in order to maximize their understanding of the linkage between the underlying values and scientific concepts. We would reason from this that although there is a need to expand the number of science concepts used to add depth and balance to discussions, the inclusion of values considerations in conservation education is also very important.

Decision-making in science classes

We now turn to attempts to incorporate discussion of socio-scientific issues into science lessons on a regular basis. This case study concentrated on four classes of 15-year-old boys in a single-sex comprehensive school in the South of England. As they followed their science course, besides being introduced to scientific concepts and relevant skills, the boys formed opinions about the applications and use of science in social contexts. This research tried to gain insights into students' deliberations as they discussed socio-scientific issues. What comments did they make? How did they interact with others? What knowledge and value base did they draw on? How did their teachers manage and support discussions?

The science department had adopted an issues-based science course – *Salters Science* – a year prior to the research. Four teachers teaching mixed-ability, but higher band, classes agreed to take part in the study. Discussions with low achieving students were thus not explored. The course consisted of 12 science units, each lasting about three weeks (about fourteen hours of lesson time). Each unit raised a societal problem which was the focus for a particular student activity (a debate, structured questions for individual response, or a role-play). For the first six units decision-making tasks were produced which were designed either to replace the existing activity with the same focus or to provide an additional task closely linked to the science content of the unit. The selection of issues had to be related to the content and activities in the modules being studied. Within these constraints, the following types of issue were included:

- *Personal and immediate*: an issue in which the task explored personal responses and proposed actions
  'What are you prepared to do to use energy more efficiently?'
  'Risky? What activities are you prepared to engage in which may carry some risk?'
- *Local and less immediate*: an issue in which opinions can be formed but any actions linked to these opinions cannot be undertaken at this stage

'Which material would you use for a replacement window frame?'

'What method(s) would you choose to transport butanone from manufacturer to customer?'

'Should an "improvement" programme for a river or a golf course go ahead?'

- *Global*: where judgements can be made but little action may result
'What could be done to help the world food problem?'

The decision-making tasks were outlined to the four teachers involved, indicating where they would fit during the unit. The tasks used the framework as described in Chapter 4 (page 80). The detail of the lesson structure was left to the individual teacher. Three of the classes rotated round three teachers, so that each teacher taught two particular modules to each of these classes. The fourth class had the same teacher for all of the modules. Two small groups in each of the four classes were randomly selected for in-depth study.

Three phases of data collection took place:

- pre-experience interviews with some boys, to explore decision-making strategies;
- following group discussions in science classes as students used the decision-making framework. This involved audio-taping of the teacher introduction, peer group discussion, teacher summary and collection of written work;
- post-experience interviews and questionnaires to explore decision-making strategies and perceptions of science and socio-scientific issues.

Decision-making in action

General findings from all the data collection and analysis have been reported elsewhere (Ratcliffe 1996, 1997, 2002). They include the following:

- Students were able to analyse the advantages and disadvantages of an issue, but not in a systematic way against criteria they identified.
- Few students were information-vigilant. Those that were, sought and used information across all tasks. Students drew on limited information about the underlying science.
- Students used a few dominant criteria as the basis for their reasoning. These included economics and perceived effectiveness of the proposed solution. Ethical and environmental considerations, appropriate to the contexts, featured but not frequently.

- Some of the students showed decision-making strategies which appeared persistent across the year and across individual and group tasks. These students had a constant underlying rationale for views on specific issues, but group discussion could moderate their opinion.

Here we concentrate on two decision-making scenarios to examine in detail features of teacher support and student interaction. We have chosen discussions about two contrasting issues – a personal issue, 'What are you prepared to do to use energy more efficiently?', and a global issue, 'What could be done to help the world food problem?'

Jack, a newly qualified teacher with a chemistry degree, taught the unit containing the 'energy conservation' discussion. Peter, an experienced teacher with a biological sciences background, taught the unit containing the 'world food problem'.

In order to show the main features of the lessons in relation to the decision-making framework, we summarize these as timelines (Figure 7.1).

Role of the teacher

In Chapter 4 (page 86) we outlined possible roles teachers could take in handling peer group discussion – neutral chair, balanced approach, stated commitment. We explore how Peter and Jack, with no previous experience of handling peer group discussion of controversial issues, matched up to features of possible roles, given that the study was conducted prior to the 1996 legislation and citizenship guidance.

Both Jack and Peter provided fairly brief introductions to the decision-making task. Jack explained that they were going to discuss energy saving as a continuation of examining heat transfer. He made reference to the worksheets (Box 7.1) and encouraged students to use the decision-making framework as suggested (Chapter 4, page 80). He seemed to have a clear understanding of the structure for decision-making, prompting students, as a whole class, to move from one part of the structure to the next at appropriate points in the lesson (Figure 7.1). Jack had little interaction with the groups once they were underway, his role appearing to be ensuring that the class generally were on-task. He tended to limit the amount of teacher talk and whole-class discussion. In contrast, Peter, as an experienced teacher with a reputation for clear control, wished to maintain a firm steer over activities. He seemed far less willing for students to engage in small group discussion, expressing fears that boys would be off-task and engaging in irrelevant discussion. His fears proved unjustified in the main (Figure 7.1), even given that students had not chosen the focus for discussion themselves. In most lessons Peter had an introduction of sufficient length to frame the task but without exploring student understanding too deeply (Box 7.2). Although he used the decision-making framework with other tasks

The first line shows the actions of the teacher with respect to the particular group of students:
T Teacher to whole class;   G teacher with group.

The second line shows the student group discussion with relation to aspects of decision-making:
O options; C criteria; I information; S survey/reasoning; D choosing with reasoning; R reviewing decision.

The third line shows student group discussion which is not related to decision-making:
p discussing procedures; u unstructured discussion; x off-task.
Each character represents ½ minute.

Energy conservation lessons led by Jack
Group A: Steve, Jim, Scott, Bob

```
Time
........5.........10........15........20........25........30........35........40........45..
Teacher:
TTTTTTTTTTTTTTT                                 GGGG      G                              TTTTTTT
Students:          OOOOOOIIIII        CC   OOOOOOIIOIIC   SS   SSSSSSSSSSSSSSSS
           PPPPPPPP            uuppppppp ppuu                  xxxx   xxx
```

Group B: Darren, Amit, Martin, Alan, Jason

```
........5.........10........15........20........25........30........35........40........45
Teacher:
TTTTTT           T   GG                      G T    GGGGTGG
Students:  IOI  OOOOOOOOOOOOOOO  OOOOSSSS  OOOOCCCCC  C    IIII II    SSSSSSSSSSSSS
           xxxxpppxx  uppp       uu        uux        uu uuuuuuu      uuxx
```

```
.......50.........55.........60.......65
         T   TTTTTTTTTTTTTTTTTTTTT

OOO   DDDDRR
x   uu
```

World food problem lessons led by Peter
Group A   Steve, Jim, Scott

```
.........5.........10.........15.........20.........25.........30.........35.........40.........45..
Teacher:
TTTTTTTTT       TTTT     TTT  GGG  TTT    TTTTTTTTTTTTTTTT                                    T
Students OOOCCIII    OOOOOOO     DDDDDDDDDDD              DDIC    DDD
                               xx         xx   pp    pppp        xxxxpppxxxxxxpp
```

Group B
Darren, Martin, Alan, Amit

```
.........5.........10.........15.........20.........25.........30.........35.........40.........45..
Teacher:
TTTTTTTTT       TTTTT    TT   TT   TTTTTTTTT
Students OOOOOOOOOOOO   DDDDDDD  IIIIIIIISSSSSSS
```

Figure 7.1 Timelines for decision-making lessons showing a summary of interaction

---

Box 7.1   Support material for 'energy conservation' and 'world food problem' discussions

---

Energy matters   ENERGY CONSERVATION

When energy sources are used inefficiently, money and precious resources are wasted. There is an energy cost to most activities we do –
*   buying and using articles which have taken a lot of energy to produce;
*   using energy sources in the home inefficiently;
*   using labour-saving devices at work and in the home.
Our standard of living can depend on the energy sources available and how we use them.
What are you prepared to do to use energy more efficiently?

This was followed by the decision-making framework. Additional information sheets showed the power rating and cost of using household electrical appliances; the estimated costs and savings of different methods of household thermal insulation.

Food for thought   WORLD FOOD PROBLEM

Is it possible to feed the world? There are 500 million people in the world without enough to eat – more than the populations of Europe and the USA put together. More than 20 million people die from causes related to hunger every year. More than 100 people will die from starvation today. How can *we* deal with this problem?
1 Write down *your* first reaction to this question.
Work in a group. Use any information sheets that are helpful

This was followed by the decision-making framework. Additional information sheets discussed the divide between rich and poor countries in terms of colonization, farming methods, land use, water and living standards.

---

during the year, when part way through the 'world food problem' he encouraged a slightly different method, despite the decision-making framework sheets given to the students (Box 7.2). In doing this, it was as if he wanted to have tight control over the purposes of the small group discussions and saw the focus as coming up with a variety of solutions. He encouraged fairly speedy decision-making. In summarizing students' views part way through the lesson, it is clear that he was trying to act as 'neutral chair', collecting students' views in an encouraging and open way but with little evaluation (Box 7.3). At first, he gathered responses which point towards 'scientific' solutions and perhaps felt on safe ground. When students moved towards 'political' solutions, he was at first encouraging in recognizing this additional dimension but then seemed

Box 7.2 Peter's introduction to the world food problem for Class A

Peter: We're going to take a break from the heavy science and revisit the original problem of the unit. Let's pull ourselves back to the original problem which was – can we feed the world? As we hinted at last time, politicians are whingeing and crying and wringing their hands saying – no, no there's too many people, you cannot do it. Well, we've learnt one or two ideas already on this subject – that scientifically at least the evidence is that it is possible to feed the world with the present population and some optimists even say it's possible to feed six times that level . . . Why is it that well over two-thirds of the population of the world goes hungry or at least malnourished – doesn't get a proper diet? That's your little discussion to enter into today – the rest of the sheet is very much open to you. Um, is it possible to feed the world, well, you know, theory says it is – but theory doesn't go into practice, so what is it that is stopping us from doing so? (reading) There are 500 million people in the world without enough to eat – more than the population of Europe and USA put together – more than 20 million people die from causes related to hunger every year. What does it mean by that? 'Causes related to hunger' – what do you think they mean?

Boy: Contracting something by not eating the right foods.

Peter: Yeh, by not eating the right food you're more likely to be malnourished – you're more likely to die of certain diseases. More than a hundred people will die from starvation today. How can we deal with the problems? Write your first reactions to these questions, and you now, you put those down – what you think your first reactions are. Um, I'm going to get each group to have a scribe. Now, get together; get into more of a huddle.

After four minutes of peer group discussion, using the framework as support, Peter interrupts.

Peter: Can I just throw out to you another way you could do this. You've all hopefully made a list, in fact if you haven't done that I'm going to ask you to do that now. Just produce a thin, narrow list, no explanations, just a thin, narrow list of all the possible ways in which we could try and solve the world food problem. In other words, problem solving. One way you can problem solve is brainstorming – so have a brainstorm . . . Let them keep coming out, go round and round – what's your idea? What's your idea? What's your idea? Go round again. Any ideas should be accepted. Do not discuss it. Do not evaluate it. Do not say – that's a stupid idea . . . Sometimes the wackiest ideas turn out to be the ones that people can develop the most. So accept, within reason, what everyone says and go round and round again. Keep saying the same question – solve the world food problem – I would . . . This is what we could do – and I'm going to give you another five minutes at the most and I want a quick lively, loud, no not too loud, discussion going round and round in tight little circles. Under the title brainstorm – five minutes. Go!

Box 7.3 Peter's discussion with Class A of possible solutions to the world food problem

---

Peter: Right, let's just whizz round the groups – whoever was not scribing – this time you'll have to make a decision. The non-scribes, one of them, can read out the main decision you've come up with. What are your main ones? (to front group)

Boy 1: Breeding crops to (inaudible)

Peter: Right, so they're saying one way to solve the world food problem is to look at improved breeding of crops so that they can grow in variety of climates. Good, next.

Boy 1: Better irrigation.

Peter: So you're using science there and then improved irrigation. You've got a third one?

Boy 2: And then, um (inaudible)

Peter: Right, so training farmers. OK.

Boy 3: (to class) To sort out wars so that money is saved and put to good use.

Peter: You mean irrigation, trying to get the water.

Boy 3: No, wars.

Peter: Oh, wars. Well done. Well done. Trying to sort out the politicians.

Boy 3: Because the fighting usually . . .

Peter: Trying to sort out politicians so you don't have so much squabbling, so much fighting over land and get on with feeding people instead.

Boy 3: And then some of the richer countries that have, like, colonized poorer countries can invest money into farming and . . .

Peter: You've gone for the political solution. Politicians trying to help out the poorer countries by putting some of the money back where they took it out once.

. . . (more solutions suggested)

Peter: Well done. So you've attacked from the individual point of view about how much we eat. We've had scientific addressing of it, political addressing of it, another science and politics over there and now we've got an individual's approach. All taken different angles – all very sound.

. . .

Boy 5: Birth control.

Peter: Ah, another solution to it. Right. Reduce the number of mouths in the first place.

Boy 6: Extermination process.

Peter: You actually voted for that one did you?

Boy 6: He did.

Boy 7: Don't accuse me.

Peter: Got daleks around? (In dalek voice) Anyone over 40 will be exterminated, exterminated. Next.

Boy 8: We decided to dig fresh water wells or fly food over.

Peter: Right, so again, better distribution of food, getting food to people and better water supplies. So, you want the drastic, reduce the number of people first and then fewer births and more deaths – from one to the other. The real humanitarian approach. And then we go for the cannibalistic approach.

Box 7.4   Steve, Jim and Scott's response to the class views

Jim: Like I said before – all the ideas could be put into operation except the extermination, though. (pause)

Steve: Why would Bob say you'd got to kill half the population?

Jim: You could run a few tests and see its powers (?)(inaudible) I suppose.

Steve: What, see how quickly we could kill . . .

Scott: They'd have to kill anyway. What Bob said he was joking but it's true isn't it?

Steve: What, send gunmen(?)(barely audible) over to the third world?

Scott: Yeh.

---

embarrassed in dealing with the unacceptable solution of 'extermination' while still acting as neutral chair. The 'neutral chair' stance can result in acceptance that any solution is valid – leaving the students to explore the morality or otherwise of different solutions, a point captured in the audio-taped group (Box 7.4).

Humanities teachers reading these extracts from Peter's lesson may see shortcomings of the discussion and Peter's approach. Shouldn't the concepts of justice, politics and world trade be more to the fore in such discussions? Shouldn't there be more opportunity than this lesson to explore such issues? How important is the understanding of the underlying science in making sense of the issue? These tensions lie at the heart of discussing socio-scientific issues. Peter was starting from a science perspective – the biology of food production – to open out discussion into the social consequences and limitations of farming methods. In doing so, he showed willingness to explore students' views and encourage them to recognize the social impact of scientific and technological advancements. However, limitations of time, curriculum scope, his stance and expertise discouraged him from exploring such issues in any depth.

Jack had perhaps the more comfortable discussion to summarize, focusing as it did more on the available scientific information than politics and justice. Nonetheless, opportunities for consideration of the impact of individuals' actions on others were under-explored. Jack had encouraged the use of the decision-making framework throughout the lesson, listening to groups' discussion rather than supporting or intervening (Figure 7.1). As a summary he asked each group to report their views on how they would save energy, with reasons (which were mostly economic). He then summarized the discussions in relation to scientific and economic arguments (Box 7.5). He moved from household energy saving into wider issues of transport, starting a wider ranging discussion but without the time to take it very far. This was typical of his summaries, in which he gave further information about the context, but limited the comments initiated by students.

Both Peter and Jack encouraged students to make their views known and generally were accepting and valuing of students' contributions. Peter and Jack each adopted his individual stance with different classes, on these and other issues. We suspect that neither had considered exactly how they would summarize the students' discussion until during the lesson. Peter maintained an approach as 'neutral chair', seeking views, with limited evaluation from each discussion group. Jack, while collecting views briefly from each group, summarized in evaluative terms, throwing in comments related to the science and his views.

The classes appeared to accept the teacher's role as that of controlling the procedures in the lesson, recognizing that student discussion allowed them to put forward their own views. There is evidence, in the audio-taped discussions from these and other teachers' classes, that the teacher's 'authority' did not extend to influencing the viewpoints students adopted. This may be a reflection of the 'neutral chair' stance and also to do with adolescents having individual perspectives which teachers' views were unlikely to change substantially. As an example we show the thwarted attempts by Trevor (one of the other two teachers) to encourage some consideration of environmental sustainability in students' individual actions (Box 7.6). This discussion alone could not shift these adolescents' egocentric approach. Teachers, in adopting mostly a role of 'neutral chair', thus had influence over procedures but not over views expressed. The potential for a more evaluative stance was present in the decision-making structure – the review of decision process – but was under-explored. This point is amplified later.

Student learning

We now turn to examine what students appeared to show in, and gain from, structured peer group discussion in this case study. The original intention of providing a structure had been to examine the extent to which this helped students in encouraging a systematic approach to considering different sides of an issue. We explore here the actions of two groups in different classes in their discussions of 'energy conservation' and the 'world food problem'. Jim, Steve, Scott and Bob formed a cohesive group in Class A. Darren, Alan, Amit and Martin were a more diverse group in Class B. We look at their interactions, use of the decision-making framework, and reasoning involved in their discussions.

Box 7.5 Jack's summary of the energy conservation discussions in Class B

Jack: It seems the things that you think are most valid in terms of energy saving costs are – insulating your loft, lagging your tank and putting aluminium foil behind radiators. That's the three things I heard and low energy light bulbs at the back there. Now, one of the reasons that the majority of people have done those things is that they tend to be the cheaper options. It doesn't actually cost a lot to do those things. Double-glazing, on the other hand, if you looked at your list, costs £1500. In terms of the energy saved, the actual costs of the energy saved rather than the actual environmental costs of using the energy, that took 30 years to pay back. That's probably one of the main reasons why the majority of houses in this country, at least, are not double-glazed. If you lived in Sweden or Canada the majority of houses are double-glazed. That's because it's so cold in those countries that the energy you do save (interrupted). The average temperature in Canada in the winter can be about minus 25, minus 30 degrees, double-glazing can be worthwhile. One of the things I noticed when I was going round that many of you were not taking into account at all was the cost in energy of producing things. If you take for example a motor car. It costs about, ooh, about a thousand pound's worth of energy to produce a motor car. We're talking about the energy costs which goes into making the steel, the plastic, transporting the car from A to B and all the rest of it.

　　This is before you take into account the amount of fuel they use. If you go into the town in rush hour and observe cars going past you'll see the vast majority contain one passenger only. So all that energy is being used to transport one person. If you looked instead at the costs of using a bus, although a bus, uses a lot more petrol or diesel it can carry a lot more people. Why do we use cars then? The reason people choose to use cars is principally convenience. How would you improve the system? How would you encourage people to use public transport?

Boy 1: Give them a free trial. Let them ride without a fare for the first week and then if they like it they'd use it.

Jack: That doesn't actually solve the problem, does it?

Boy 2: Make it easier.

Jack: That's it, make it cheaper, easier, put more buses on maybe

(more inaudible discussion along these lines)

Boy 3: They're using electricity now.

Boy 4: They're using vegetable oil

(noises of disbelief)

Boy 4: They are. Sir, isn't that true, Sir? (Jack, elsewhere, dismissing groups)

Box 7.6 Trevor's attempts to encourage consideration of individual action in students' decision-making about choice of material for window frames

---

In the summary discussion, Trevor asks one group their views after he has spent a little time with the group trying to explain how individual action can accumulate.

Boy 1: Well we thought we'd go for uPVC 'cos it's quality and if you buy the softwood you've got to keep maintaining it. It would cost more and you'd probably end up paying as much as you'd pay for the uPVC anyway – so you might as well buy that.

Trevor: Did the environmental effects have any bearing on your decision?

Boy 2: A little bit.

Boy 3: Yeh a little bit, (sotto voce) just a tad.

Trevor: So that helped sway you away from hardwood?

Boy 3: Oh yeh but we still think just cutting down one more tree for our bedroom window's not going to make that much difference.

Trevor: OK, do you all agree with that?

Boy 1: Yeh.

Trevor: You didn't take my points about you're just a drop in the ocean but with lots of other drops have a large effect?

Boy 3: Oh yes we considered that but (interrupted by others – issue not returned to).

The timelines (Figure 7.1) show that procedural interactions formed an early part of the discussions for both groups in using the framework for 'energy conservation'. Some of these were concerned with one or more students taking the lead in determining the direction of discussion. In Group A, Jim seemed the dominant and information-vigilant leader (in 'energy conservation': 'Right, let's go. Shall we begin. I suggest we elect a chair'; 'Shut up, please, we'll only have sensible contributions'). Group B were more egalitarian but Martin most frequently took the initiative in taking the discussion forward (in 'energy conservation': 'Let's just get on. Write down your first reactions to the question'; 'Right. Information. Do you have useful information about each option?'; 'Shall we write? We've checked our information').

Space does not allow us to show all the details of the discussions. The timelines (Figure 7.1) show that in the 'energy conservation' discussion, where Jack encouraged systematic use of the decision-making framework, both groups used all parts of the framework, except review. Criteria, the basis for any decision, were only discussed briefly before engaging in a relatively unsystematic survey of the possibilities. In the 'world food problem' where the teacher, Peter, effectively discouraged overt identification of criteria, some discussion was had about possible solutions and their rationale. Review and evaluation of reasoning, although encouraged in the framework, was only cursorily addressed, if at all, by any group.

We present extracts which capture the main decisions, and their reasons, which were shown by the groups (Box 7.7). These extracts do not convey the nuances of reasoning shown during group discussion but represent the prevailing views by the end of the lesson. The extracts illustrate the rather different nature of the two issues. 'Energy conservation' was seen as closely linked with the science topic. The decision-making structure appeared to help students consider the options somewhat systematically, with students sharing their views and arguments, though not very deeply. In the 'world food problem', in contrast, the lack of encouragement to consider carefully the basis for the decision and the very complex nature of the problem promoted oversimplified solutions. Although the students, in tackling a global issue, showed some appreciation of the social and political factors affecting the problem, it was difficult to judge the extent to which they identified with the issue. The 'energy conservation' discussion was intended to be closer to their experience. But even here the discussion appeared to proceed in the abstract – that is, students reasoned and made decisions as if it would have no effect on their behaviour. Thus in both cases, the discussion, as framed, may help in forming and clarifying attitudes and opinions, but appears to have little impact, as perhaps anticipated, on behaviour.

Review of decisions

A missing step from most discussions within this research was a systematic review of the decision-making process. The framework was intended to help students clarify their reasoning about possible solutions to a socio-scientific problem. Thus, the final step, reviewing the process, was felt to be crucial in evaluating the decision-making process. There may be at least two reasons why this step was omitted. An obvious one was the lack of time – many teachers, in giving students sufficient time for peer group discussion, found themselves limited in the time they had to summarize. However, even with willing and able teachers there was a reluctance to review the process. Perhaps they saw closure of the lesson in terms of a conventional science lesson – that is, coming to a consensus. Perhaps the chore of going over discussions again proved a disincentive to both students and teachers. Whatever the reason, although the intention was to develop systematic reasoning about issues, the structure was only partially successful.

Claims have been made for improved decision-making using normative structures as teaching aids over short time periods, but based on self-reporting mechanisms rather than external evaluation (Mann *et al.* 1988). Repeated use of the decision-making framework did not add greatly to students' skills in its use nor to their recognition that here was a structure to assist them in systematic reasoning (interview evidence). Consideration of socio-scientific issues

Box 7.7   Decisions made in the peer group discussions

Energy conservation Group A

Teacher (Jack): OK gentlemen, we'll go round and ask each group what they've discovered and what their views are.

Steve: (hurriedly) Which one are we going to choose?

Jim: Choose . . .

Scott: Loft insulation.

Jim: All of them.

Steve: Yeh.

Scott: Loft insulation.

Jim: Loft insulation. Heat rises so that would be the most overall form of insulation.

Energy conservation Group B

Martin: (reading) which option do you choose? You have made your decision.

Jason: What are we doing, loft insulation?

Darren: Yeh.

Amit: Saves a lot of money, each year, each year.

Martin: Saves 100 pound a year and also doesn't cost as much as cavity filled walls to install.

World food problem Group A

Teacher (Peter): What did you say was the best decision you could come up with?

Scott: Food should be distributed evenly.

Teacher: Even distribution of food. Good and bad points about that?

Scott: Transport costs a lot.

Teacher: Transport costing problems, yeh.

Scott: And during a war, um, when battle's on it's difficult.

Jim: (quietly) It would be difficult to transport.

Scott: Difficult getting through.

Steve: (quietly) Ambushed, get ambushed.

Teacher: These are not easy things to talk about.

World food problem Group B

Martin: What do you think?

Alan: Give the poor their own land and . . .

Amit: Foreign aid.

Martin: (pause) That is foreign aid.

Darren: I reckon the other one should be – do not give too much food to animals.

Alan: That's what I reckon.

Martin: That's what I say.

Darren: What about you Amit?

Amit: Yes, all right then.

Martin: Give back land to poor or help poor. Put that under the same heading as foreign aid.

can aid decision-making skills as long as these skills are explicitly practised and evaluated (Aikenhead 1994). We suggest that systematic reflection is an integral element of any decision-making strategy. Its neglect was unfortunate. One way to address this lack of reflection is perhaps to evaluate the decisions of others (Chapter 4, page 79).

Summary

In these case studies, students valued peer group discussion and used the decision-making framework as a guide. Discussions were dominated by clarification of values but informed implicitly, and sometimes explicitly, by a limited number of scientific concepts. The discussions could moderate students' initial views but not necessarily influence or change their actions. In both global issues and more local ones where action might be possible, there seemed little discussion and development of responsibility and the impact of individuals' actions on others. This is not necessarily surprising given the focus on sharing opinions. These case studies have provided some insight into the limited level of scientific knowledge used within the classroom context. Overt recognition by the teacher of the scientific knowledge likely to inform a particular socio-scientific issue, and communication of this to students, may provide a firmer scientific base. Decision-making tasks have both strengths and limitations. They encourage discussion of socio-scientific issues in a systematic way but require careful explanation of the purposes of the discussion and decision-making structure. Perhaps only with direction from the teacher in evaluating and reflecting on the decision-making process will students gain good procedural understanding of their decision-making.

8 Community projects

This chapter uses a community project, involving teacher collaboration, to discuss a holistic approach to a socio-scientific issue. The *MIDAS* project (Making Informed Decisions About Sustainability) was funded by the Worldwide Fund for Nature (WWF-UK). It provided a means of delivering education for sustainable development (ESD) through the science curriculum, involving primary and secondary schools, and local community groups with an interest in the selected sustainability issues.

Collaboration was central to the project as a key aim was to bridge the work between primary and secondary schools in Southampton involving the local community. Meaningful work on progression between primary and secondary schools necessarily involves active collaboration between primary and secondary school teachers. Meaningful sustainable development education (as discussed in Chapter 2) should include consideration of real issues, of relevance to students' lives, and this requires collaboration with other interest groups (stakeholders) from the local community. It is clear from the start that in projects of this nature, considerable attention is paid to managing the people and processes involved. We therefore provide a description of the 'journey' taken by the project, and by the partners as they strive to meet their individual objectives. We discuss the general difficulties encountered, the solutions found, and positive – sometimes unexpected – outcomes.

Implementation

An overview of the project's learning activities for 11- and 13-year-old students is shown in Table 8.1 to put the subsequent discussion into context. The activities themselves are not discussed in detail here, but they centre round a fieldwork component, which is in our view crucial to any community project. This involved first-hand experience of the local environment – lakes in the city around which the local sustainable development issues (feeding ducks and fishing) revolved.

Table 8.1   Outline of the sequence of project activities, with associated learning goals (as identified in Chapter 3).

	Activities	Learning goals
Pre-fieldwork activities:	Students' 'worldviews' on issues that concern them	Clarification of personal values
	Activities raising general environmental/ sustainability matters – based on existing school and government schemes of work Group activity discussing 'good' and 'bad' reasons for fishing/feeding ducks	Scientific endeavour Scope of the issue Science concepts Science concepts Evidence evaluation Ethical reasoning Interaction of personal and social values
Fieldwork activities:	Earth Education activities (based on activities from Cornell 1989; and Van Matre 1990)	Scope of the issue Science concepts Evidence evaluation Ethical reasoning Interaction of personal and social values
	Duck-feeding (11-year-olds) and fishing (13-year-olds) activities – focusing on science and sustainable development issues	Scientific endeavour Scope of the issue Science concepts
Post-fieldwork activities:	Analysing data collected in the field	Scientific endeavour Evidence evaluation
	Discussing duck-feeding/fishing as sustainability issues Decision-making activity Role-play activity Survey of students' views and understanding of sustainable development issues	These activities can address all learning goals depending on the emphasis given by the teacher

Why include a fieldwork component?

There is a wealth of literature supporting the value of fieldwork in promoting lifelong environmental, social and personal awareness and attitudes, and there are claims that childhood and adolescent experiences with nature are a key factor in developing adult attitudes toward the environment (e.g. Eagles and Demare 1999). Positive outcomes now closely connected with citizenship programmes, such as enhanced self-esteem, self-confidence and communication skills, have been attributed to outdoor education (Cooper 1994), and children who underachieve in the classroom often excel at outdoor activities (Freeman 1995). But outdoor education is not without its critics. Evidence of a correlation between early experience and attitudes or behaviour later in life is very difficult to demonstrate due to the complex and long-term nature of this type of research (Chawla 1999). Many authors (e.g. Van Matre 1990; Simmons 1994) argue that it is unlikely that children will develop a more positive environmental ethic through a single fieldtrip in a natural setting, because such experiences have little relevance to their everyday lives, and they are not able to transfer what they have learnt from the experience back to their home settings. However, a study by Simmons (1994) found that children responded best in settings that are familiar to them, and other studies suggest that children's experience with the environment should begin with their local area (Simpson 1985; Neal and Palmer 1990). The focus for the present study took this research evidence into consideration in promoting an activity coincident with the objectives within the science curriculum.

Why focus on progression?

Recent reports have shown that continuity in the curriculum and progression in learning as students move from primary to secondary school (at age 11 in England) are major weaknesses of the English education system (Ofsted 2002a, 2002b). There are considerable personal and social implications of transferring from primary to secondary school, and these aspects are generally managed more successfully than developing curriculum continuity or common teaching approaches. Research based on interviews and lesson observations in 32 primary and their 16 partner secondary schools revealed that partner schools '. . . generally had little knowledge of their respective practices in assessing and recording progress and in setting targets', and '. . . there was insufficient discussion between [primary and secondary school] teachers . . . about the standards of work expected and about approaches to teaching' (Ofsted 2002b: 2). This report suggests that teachers need more opportunity to observe and discuss teaching in each other's schools to help bridge the gap. With specific regard to teaching about environmental and sustainable development matters, there are now government schemes of work available that can be modified and linked together to support progression and continuity (QCA 2002).

Interaction of teachers and other partners

Building the project partnership
There are a number of non-governmental organizations (NGOs) which provide an informal approach to teaching about sustainability issues and, although these can be effective, their programmes are often very different from those within the formal school curriculum. Previous experience showed us that there

is such a diversity of approaches that it would be inefficient to call a meeting of all potential educational interest groups to sort out a mechanism for achieving the project's objectives. A better approach was to build the partnership slowly, beginning with teachers, who are the people closest to the everyday education of the individual students. The most straightforward way to assist and track progression effectively was first to involve a secondary school in the city, and then contact its 'feeder' primary schools. Once these had been recruited, local community groups with a track record of working closely with schools and children were contacted, and the first meeting was held to agree objectives, approaches and priorities. From the priorities agreed at this meeting, other potential partners with relevant expertise and experience were then contacted.

Project partners fell into four main categories: the university (from the teacher training and educational research perspectives); the schools; the local community partners; and the WWF.

> *University involvement*: Two staff from the University of Southampton, one primary science and one secondary science educator, attended meetings and supported the project throughout. Trainee teachers at the university (75 primary and 50 secondary) took part in the field activities and helped evaluate the work.
>
> *School involvement*: One urban secondary school and two of its 'feeder' primary schools were involved in the project, one large and one small. 120 secondary students took part, and 180 primary students – which constituted whole year groups. Key staff at each of these schools, science specialists, were involved throughout the project.
>
> *Community group involvement*: Over the life of the project, community group representation ebbed and flowed. Groups' involvement and interest in the project invariably depended on the energy and interests of individuals. Two types of community groups were involved:
>
> - 'Umbrella' groups that tend to have a broad environmental/ sustainability remit within the area. These included: the city sustainability forum; the county environmental education group; the city local education authority; city community action groups and Local Agenda 21 officers; the urban wildlife centre.
> - More local groups with a narrower focus in terms of location or interest, which included: local residents' associations; the 'friends' of Southampton Common group; the local pond conservation group; school parents' and teachers' associations; local historical associations; local fishing tackle shops; local angling clubs; local 'mother and toddler' groups.

Defining and agreeing project objectives

The immediate challenge faced by partners in a new project is to agree common interests and objectives, and this challenge deepens when the partnership includes members from diverse backgrounds, as in this case. Everyone involved has different interests and priorities, and these need exploring from the start in order to agree the way ahead – which must inevitably involve compromises by all concerned. In this project, for example, the schools' objectives were largely developmental, focusing on products in the form of teaching materials, whereas the university's objectives were more research-oriented. The community partners' objectives were a combination of these depending on their individual area of expertise.

Exploring and agreeing the objectives of education for sustainable development was the first priority for the project partnership. After reading several of the numerous definitions and suggestions, they finally agreed to work towards achieving at least some of the seven 'key concepts of sustainable development' proposed by the Sustainable Development Education Panel (see Box 2.2, page 33). The seven key concepts include familiar school science concepts such as interdependence and diversity, but also some not traditionally recognized as part of science education, such as citizenship, quality of life, equity and justice – areas which many science teachers are still doubtful about teaching (Grace and Sharp 2000a). For the school partners the main concern was deciding which of the key concepts could be realistically addressed by the project, and linking these with relevant government schemes of work (QCA 2002).

Selecting an appropriate sustainability theme and activities

Given the multi-faceted nature of sustainable development, it was important for the project to maintain a tight focus and have clear learning objectives. At the first project meeting, partners agreed to focus on issues surrounding the varied, and often conflicting, interests people have in the city lakes, to appreciate these, and to see how science can help to clarify some of these issues. Aspects of sustainable development can be addressed through issues such as angling, duck feeding, conservation of water and wildlife, and rats and disease.

Three-quarters of Britain's ponds have been lost over the last hundred years and many are now threatened by pollution and mismanagement. Ponds have significant local historic, amenity and biodiversity importance, and action is vital to ensure that further losses are prevented. We all have views about how our local ponds should be used – but these views are not always the same! Particularly contentious issues are the impact that feeding ducks (Box 8.1) and fishing (Box 8.2) have on the local wildlife. At first sight, the issues may seem like variations on traditional science investigations, i.e. addressing the question 'How does fishing/feeding the ducks affect local wildlife in and around the lake?' However, the question can be reworded and extended into a socio-scientific (sustainability) context to ask 'What should be done about fishing/

Box 8.1   Feeding ducks as a sustainability issue

Year 6. Theme: What should be done about duck feeding on the Common?
Feeding the ducks on the Common is a very real and controversial issue, although most children (and possibly adults too) may be unaware of this. (In fact a local park warden recently had a heated argument on this site with a local resident who habitually collects all the bread left over at the local supermarket at the end of each day and unloads it into the lake for the ducks!) Almost all children have fed the ducks here at some time in their lives, and it is a popular pastime for many children and adults alike. However, the activity has increased to the extent that 'bread-slicks' are sometimes seen at the edge of the lake when the ducks are simply unable to eat any more. There are the consequent environmental concerns such as eutrophication, reduced biodiversity, increased disease, and increased populations of rats and scavenging birds; but these are also social concerns as they directly affect everyone who uses the lake. The ramifications of this can be explored further with older students by, for example, encouraging critical enquiry and trying to find answers to a long list of 'scientifically-oriented' and 'socially oriented' questions such as:

- Who feeds the ducks on the lake? – and why?
- What kind of food do they give to the ducks?
- What do wild ducks normally eat?
- Are some kinds of foods better than others – health-wise, environmentally, aesthetically?
- When does this activity go on?
- What will happen to the bread that is not eaten?
- If the ducks eat mouldy food what will happen to them?
- What will the rats and crows (and ducks) eat when bread is not available?
- Does the activity affect natural wildlife populations? How can we show this?
- How might the activity promote disease among wildlife and people?
- Who else uses the lake? How does the activity affect them? What are their views?

And ultimate decision-making questions such as:
- What should be done about the situation, and how?

---

feeding the ducks on the lake?' Students would need to consider the first question in order to address the second question properly. They would need to appreciate that this is an area of conflict, involving different interest groups with different views, and they would need to undertake scientific investigations in order to help make decisions about the validity and reliability of these views.

This local lake sustainability theme was finally agreed because it fulfilled the following criteria:

- It is a *real* issue involving real conflicts of interest.
- It is *local* to all schools.
- It is a familiar and accessible theme to all students. Just about all children (in Southampton and elsewhere) have visited ponds and lakes at some time.
- It is readily adaptable by schools in other areas, as ponds and lakes are frequently found in both rural and urban public open spaces.
- Sustainable development has long been included in the geography

---

Box 8.2   Fishing as a sustainability issue

Angling is one of the most popular leisure activities in Britain, and a very lucrative business. With people's main leisure time and even livelihoods involved, the suggestion that fishing should be banned or even moderated can be highly contentious. It may be true that many anglers are unaware of the environmental, health and social consequences of the activity, but perhaps this is partly because such matters are not considered at school.

It is important to bear in mind that there are different kinds of anglers: people take up fishing for a variety of reasons, each resulting in different types of behaviour. At one extreme, there are those whose goal may be to relax and enjoy the natural environment regardless of whether they catch a fish. At another extreme there are people who are intent on catching the most or the biggest fish as quickly as possible, and this may involve introducing certain breeds, feeding fish with particular bait, removing marginal vegetation, and possibly leaving hooks, weights and twine in the vicinity.

As with duck feeding in Box 8.1, the issue can be explored further by attempting to find answers to critical questions such as:

- Who fishes on the lake – and why do they do it?
- What kind of bait do they give the fish?
- What do natural fish populations normally eat?
- Are some kinds of foods better than others – health-wise, environmentally, aesthetically?
- When does this activity go on?
- What are the consequences of discarding bait, hooks, weights, twine, etc?
- Does the activity affect natural animal and plant populations? How can we show this?
- How might the activity promote disease among wildlife and people?
- Who else uses the lake? How does the activity affect them? What are their views?

And ultimate decision-making questions such as:
- What should be done about the situation, and how?

curriculum, but only more recently in the science curriculum, where there are still relatively few teaching materials.

Using the theme of city ponds and lakes as a focus for both primary and secondary classes helped to secure curriculum continuity and progression in learning among students. An appropriate theme for primary students was an investigation of duck feeding and sustainability (Box 8.1). Secondary students looked at the theme of fishing and sustainability (Box 8.2). Enquiry into either of these issues can provide opportunities to carry out some scientific research and also explore ways of measuring people's attitudes and behaviour – i.e. address the learning goals we have previously discussed in relation to socio-scientific issues (see Chapter 3, page 40).

Project outcomes

Outcomes for partners

Positive outcomes for school partners

Teachers agreed that many of the benefits of working together were often feelings rather than quantifiable outcomes. However, partners were unanimously agreed on the following positive outcomes:

- The teaching experience and the materials developed provided clearer progression in learning about sustainability between primary and secondary school, and clarified links between science and sustainable development.
- Involvement in the project provided a chance to step back and reflect on the issues and how best to teach them.
- Peer observation – watching each other in a teaching situation with the students – was a useful experience in itself to appreciate that there are different, yet equally effective ways of teaching the same thing. Primary and secondary teachers worked together during the field-work, and visited each other's schools to observe and join in the project classroom activities.
- It was apparent that teaching the students outside the classroom (and off the school site) required different teaching skills, and these were only fully appreciated through first-hand experience.
- From the secondary teachers' point of view, this was an opportunity to get to know the students who would soon be coming up to their school.
- There was some genuine surprise among the secondary teachers at the considerable amount of science covered during the primary classes. This is not always evident simply by reading primary curriculum documents.

- The project rekindled ideas about a 'science club' for local primary and secondary students, although this kind of initiative greatly depends on the enthusiasm of individual teachers. Plans are now in place for some students to work together on the project as part of a local 'peer educator' initiative.

Positive outcomes for community partners

Simple fliers for the project were sent to coordinators of potential community action groups across the city. The initial response was small, but there was particular interest from one city ward. However, there was increasing interest from community groups and individuals as the project became more widely acknowledged. A public meeting about the use and abuse of local lakes was held at the university, which stimulated interest from all across the city, including press and radio coverage. This also gave the students an opportunity to present findings to the local community, helping to raise the school and project profile. As the project came to a close, the materials were incorporated into the local 'Healthy Schools Project', which is a nationwide government-funded initiative, thus enabling some of the materials and ideas to be disseminated more widely.

The project was an opportunity to encourage local schools and students to take more responsibility for their actions in the community; to raise awareness of their place in the community, and awareness of other existing projects. Individuals and community groups are beginning to see the potential value of linking with their local schools to help improve the local environment, and supporting national curriculum project work such as this. The benefits are long-term and can be difficult to appreciate in the early stages. However, the public meeting about the use and abuse of local ponds stimulated debate and strengthened links between the community and the schools, and strengthened their collective resolve to prioritize local sustainability issues.

Positive outcomes for university partners

The project provided a chance to work with people outside the university, explore local interest and expertise in education for sustainable development, appreciate the practicalities of implementing such a project, and produce useful training materials for trainee teachers. The project ensured that all trainee science teachers, primary and secondary, gained the outdoor leadership award, and became familiar with the materials by spending a whole day teaching groups of children out in the field. An important training tool here was to encourage the trainees to team-teach the materials, sometimes in mixed primary–secondary teams.

Barriers to implementation and possible solutions

Besides problematic aspects of building the project team, there were other barriers. We report here some of the other difficulties encountered and some solutions found, in the hope that managers of other comparable projects are able to avoid or solve similar problems. Depending on the 'success criteria' chosen for a project of this kind, issues can either be viewed as barriers to advancement, or as part of the learning challenge intrinsic to such a project.

i   *Time considerations*

The project was slow to take off and develop, despite regular meetings. It took a surprisingly long time (about six months) to develop the required working relationship to get the project running. Even primary and secondary science education specialists need time to agree the way forward. This very necessary lead-in period for the 'meeting of minds' should not be underestimated.

ii   *Establishing ground rules*

Agreeing ground rules at the beginning of the work, such as the allocation of the budget and roles and responsibilities, is of course fundamental to any project. We found that a crucial ground rule to establish at the start of this project was the balance between sticking to specific themes and objectives, and allowing developments to emerge as new people come into the project. These two approaches have the respective advantages of focus, communicability and greater ability to meet stated objectives within the time available, against the advantage of adapting to people's real needs, situations and enthusiasms. The project partnership agreed to a compromise between the two approaches, which was productive but risky. Using such a strategy largely depends upon the individuals involved, and the size and complexity of the project.

iii   *Cost*

The cost of hiring buses to transport the students to the sites was considerably more than anticipated, (and the extensive use of buses is questionable for an environmental project!). This led to teachers studying local maps of the area to seek out alternative study sites – this was obvious, but never previously considered, and resulted in the discovery of two excellent sites with lakes which were walkable from the schools!

iv   *Expertise and personnel*

- Changes in personnel. Five of the original ten partners have had to leave the project. All moved to other jobs, and the partnership had to adjust accordingly.
- Issues specific to teaching partners included: (i) negotiating time

away from school with the headteacher; (ii) when attending project meetings meant that their lessons needed covering, there
were associated feelings of 'guilt' or concern that their students'
learning would be disrupted; (iii) justifying to themselves and
colleagues the importance of the project to the school; (iv) lack
of awareness of relevance of ESD as part of the science curriculum; (v) the need for mutual support between teachers on the
project.

- The local education authority insists that a high proportion of
  teachers involved in off-site activities with children should have
  a standard outdoor leadership award. The partnership was surprised to find that most teachers did not have this qualification,
  so all teachers and trainee teachers were properly trained just
  prior to the fieldwork.

v   *Community partners*

- Getting the community involved demands a great amount of
  effort and perseverance because of lack of interest by some community groups. It is useful to present the issue to these groups
  from their own point of view. In this case, the pond and lakes
  theme was of little interest to the local residents' groups until we
  presented the project in terms of the specific and familiar problem of local rat infestations that could be enhanced by feeding
  the ducks.

- There are a surprising number of local organizations and initiatives to draw on and link with; but the time it takes to discover
  and contact these should not be underestimated.

Outcome for students

We now turn to exploring the impact of the community project on students'
learning.

Students' concerns

In order to locate the importance of socio-scientific issues among the students,
in relation to other aspects of their lives, we asked them all (plus some 15-year-
olds from the same secondary school) to write down three things that generally worry them (things that they would like to see changed or stopped), and
three things that would worry them if they were changed or stopped. We
elicited answers before making any reference to the environment or sustainability at all. This approach has been used successfully by other authors (Cade
1990; Bonnett and Williams 1998) with children of a comparable age, to gauge
environmental opinions. We categorized their responses as a 'personal',
'social' or 'environmental' opinion. These are obviously overlapping categor-

ies, but provided an indication of students' worldviews. We loosely defined 'environmental', 'social' and 'personal' statements as those apparently selected because they have an adverse affect on the environment, society or the individual respectively.

Table 8.2 summarizes the responses of three age groups – what generally worries them, things that they would like to see changed or stopped. The findings, from this relatively small sample of city-dwelling children, indicate that worries about environmental issues increase with age – being raised by about a third of 11-year-olds, about half of 13-year-olds, and well over half of 15-year olds. There is also an indication that girls are more likely to mention environmental issues than boys across the age ranges, but this gender difference is particularly noticeable among the older students. Previous research has shown consistently that girls tend to have a more positive attitude towards environmental issues (e.g. Morris and Schagen 1996; Grace and Sharp 2000b). Social issues are mentioned by between two-thirds and three-quarters of the boys and girls at all ages, whereas personal issues appear to become less prevalent with age.

Table 8.3 shows, in rank order, the top ten issues raised according to age and gender. This was a measure of the issues of most concern to these youngsters, and provided us with a starting point for designing sustainable development teaching programmes which have real significance to the lives of the individuals. The table shows that the importance of issues did vary with age and sex and we would argue that it is therefore useful to identify youngsters' concerns at different stages in their development. However, a good science education for citizenship programme should begin to identify the links between these issues, to help youngsters draw them together and clarify their own worldviews, recognize their own place in the world and the impact they have on it. We need to be aware of their hopes and fears in order to connect them fully with the meaning of citizenship.

Table 8.2 Main concerns among students (total percentages across each age range exceed 100 as some students expressed more than one type of concern)

Age	% expressing environmental concerns		% expressing social concerns		% expressing personal concerns	
	boys	girls	boys	girls	boys	girls
11 (n = 91)	26	38	74	72	62	89
13 (n = 92)	43	61	67	69	37	40
15 (n = 47)	57	87	68	72	23	21

Table 8.3   The top ten issues of concern raised among students (in rank order)

Age 11		Age 13		Age 15	
Boys	Girls	Boys	Girls	Boys	Girls
Family	Family	War	Family	War	Family
War	Friends	Family	Friends	Family	Friends
Television/ computers	Food/ sweets	Bullying	War	Disease	Poverty
Money	School/ exams	Friends	Bullying	Friends	War
Food/sweets	Sport	Sport	Racism	Sport	Crime
School/exams	War	Crime	Animal welfare	Poverty	Pollution
Bullying	Animal welfare	Drugs/ alcohol	Food/ sweets	Medical advances	Extinction
Pollution	Pets	Traffic congestion	Sport	Death	Global warming
Sport	Drugs	Animal welfare	Pollution	Independence/ freedom	Independence/ freedom
Drugs	Bullying	Pollution	School/ exams	Education	Sport

We should remember that in any survey such as this, older children are more able to articulate their concerns, and likely to state more detailed, sophisticated concepts, and that the responses may well be influenced by exposure to recent news items. It is also worth noting that the number of 15-year-olds mentioning personal concerns actually surprised their teachers who had assumed that they would be too self-conscious to admit to them, although an element of this might have slightly skewed the findings. The anonymity of the questionnaires and knowing that they would be analysed by a third party possibly eased students into writing their true feelings.

Students' views about the specific sustainability issues
As a simple measure of how the students' views on feeding the ducks (primary students) or fishing (secondary students) changed as a result of the community project activities, they were asked to what extent they agreed with the statement: 'Feeding the ducks/fishing on the lake should be banned.' Answers were given on a five-point scale and average results are shown in Table 8.4.

The views of both 11- and 13-year-olds were typically polarized before the activities, particularly among the younger students. After the programme they were less certain and possibly more open to an informed decision-making

Table 8.4 Percentages of 11- and 13-year-old students showing different views on banning duck-feeding and fishing respectively, before and after the project activities

Views on banning activity	11-year-olds		13-year-olds	
	Before	After	Before	After
Strongly agree	21	7	7	4
Agree	9	12	2	2
Neither agree or disagree	11	41	51	72
Disagree	5	17	4	18
Strongly disagree	54	23	36	4

exercise such as that suggested in Chapter 4. Students' comments reflected this. After the activities, students often commented that banning the practice would depend on the precise circumstances, and that they would need more information in order to make a decision; whereas before the activities, comments like these were not being made.

Students were asked to comment on positive and negative aspects of the project and they were mostly enthusiastic about the activities, particularly the fieldwork which clearly had some novelty value. Something that several younger students raised was their appreciation of the opportunity to work alongside older children.

Students' learning about general sustainability issues

To look for any medium-term effects of the community project, the students who took part during the final year of primary school were given a questionnaire when they reached secondary school. Non-project participants in the same year group also took part in the survey as the control group. Questions were related to the Sustainable Development Education Panel's seven key concepts of sustainable development (see Chapter 2, Box 2.2). The findings of this fairly brief survey indicated that students involved in the project seemed to show more reasoned views on the key concepts of sustainable development in comparison with the control group.

Summary

It has not been possible here to provide all the details of the 'roller-coaster' journey this project has taken, but hopefully it has given an impression of the barriers encountered in such collaborative projects, and possible means of overcoming them; more importantly, it has highlighted the benefits of taking a holistic approach to addressing socio-scientific issues. Students were able to address a wide range of learning goals through this project, in terms of conceptual knowledge, procedural knowledge, and attitudes and beliefs. The work also revealed that teachers have very limited knowledge about the multi-faceted, far-reaching nature of education for sustainable development (and in retrospect they were willing to admit this). There is a common perception among many teachers that ESD is environmental education, in the sense of teaching students about the environment and human impact on the environment. It takes time for science teachers to believe that there is a need to explore the social, moral, cultural and spiritual aspects of socio-scientific issues with children. It is therefore very important for project partners to spend considerable time discussing ESD among themselves, agreeing definitions, objectives and ground rules, before embarking on the work itself.

Project partners outside the school environment have limited understanding of the curricular and time constraints within which teachers work. It may seem obvious that children should be learning about responsible citizenship, but teachers have to justify its inclusion by checking where it fits with their own subject curriculum orders, and if it does not fit, there is considerable pressure on them to leave it out. Such factors contribute to a considerable and often unexpected time-lag effect on community-based projects. It takes much more time than expected to get the partnership up to speed and really to see the value of the work. This partnership-building phase appears to be entirely necessary as it simply takes people time to appreciate each other's strengths and approaches to group work, as well as their individual foibles and varied senses of humour! But once this is accomplished, the substantial benefits of this holistic approach to tackling socio-scientific issues soon become apparent, and we hope others can be encouraged to embark on similar collaborative projects.

We consider that the benefits and issues in this cross-phase collaborative project are mirrored in cross-curricular projects. Thus, taking a whole-school approach to socio-scientific issues can generate comparable advantages of sharing teaching strategies, recognizing the strengths of others' approaches and developing an influential holistic approach.

9 Effective teaching for the future

In this chapter we summarize the messages for effective teaching stemming from review of the research case studies. We also consider the implications for future teaching and learning of socio-scientific issues.

Effective teaching

Knowledge and understanding

In discussing the nature of socio-scientific issues, and learning related to them, we have implied that teachers need a good understanding of the dimensions and scope of socio-scientific issues in order to assist students in reaching the appropriate learning goals. To expect any one teacher to have a good under-standing of all of the following may be unrealistic:

- the nature of science;
- the nature of citizenship, social justice, democratic frameworks;
- the nature of media reporting;
- ethical analysis and decision-making strategies;
- probability and risk-benefit analysis;
- sustainable development;
- underlying scientific concepts at the level of scientific researchers.

We have not attempted to provide a complete education in these elements in this volume. However, realizing where an individual teacher's strengths and weaknesses lie in relation to knowledge and understanding is one step to effective teaching.

We suggest the following as useful sources to augment understanding:

The nature of science and students' understanding – Driver *et al.* (1996) give an accessible introduction to the nature of science as well as evaluating progression in understanding.

Nature of citizenship – Heater (1999) has an authoritative summary of concepts, while Osler (2000) and Crick (2000) provide discussion of citizenship concepts in relation to the introduction of citizenship education in the UK. Solomon (1992c) provides a very readable introduction, intended for post-16 students, in the context of socio-scientific issues.

The nature of media reporting – Philo's (1998) book brings together the key research findings of the Glasgow Media Group over the last 10 years and provides a valuable introduction to the whole issue of media reporting. It examines the production, content and reception of media messages.

Nature of ethics and ethical analysis – Warnock's (2001) short book is an accessible introduction to ethics. Fullick and Ratcliffe (1996) have a chapter on the nature of ethics written by an ethicist as well as providing an introduction to how ethical analysis can be conducted in the classroom

Probability and risk analysis – The British Medical Association (1990) and The Royal Society (1992) show detailed background to the use of risk information in many social contexts. Brignell (2000) takes a personal perspective in reviewing the use and abuse of probability statistics in a wide variety of contexts including socio-scientific issues.

Sustainable development – Palmer (1998) gives a useful overview of the direction that environmental education has been taking in recent times and how it is evolving into education for sustainable development. Huckle and Sterling (1997) provide an accessible collection of chapters on sustainability from the point of view of schools, government and business.

Science concepts – An overview of common misconceptions in understanding science concepts is provided by Driver et al. (1994)

Pedagogical expertise

Lack of detailed understanding of the elements of socio-scientific issues is not necessarily a bar to effective teaching. Lack of *realization* of the extent of your understanding is. Of great importance is appropriate pedagogical knowledge and skill. For example, research has explored how teachers modify their practice to teach explicitly aspects of the nature of science. Teachers who were seen as effective in promoting students' learning showed a number of attributes (Bartholomew *et al.* 2002). They were able to set clear learning goals which they shared with students and were willing to develop and support students' discussion. We consider that being to the right in the dimensions shown in Figure 9.1 encourages more understanding and participation on behalf of the students.

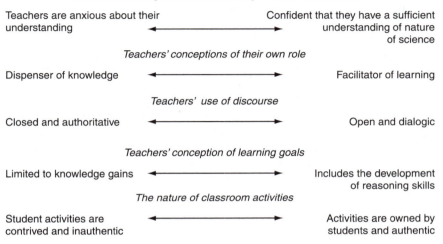

Figure 9.1 Dimensions of practice seen in teaching the nature of science

We have suggested learning strategies which encourage peer discussion and evaluation, authenticity and ownership (Chapter 4). Evaluation of some of these learning strategies in practice has illustrated the advantages and challenges to the teacher in adopting them (Chapters 5–8). Details shown in our case studies are consistent with other explorations of curriculum innovation. Lumpe *et al.* (1998), using a sample of teachers sensitized to socio-scientific issues, found that teachers saw advantages of implementation as providing motivation and meaningful applications; assisting students as decision-making citizens; using everyday materials to provide direct experiences; learning science concepts. Teachers saw disadvantages as socio-scientific issues taking more time; covering less content; having to change ways of teaching; dealing with controversial issues.

The issue of pedagogical change for the individual teacher is implied in most 'science and citizenship' curriculum approaches and is recognized in many studies of curriculum innovation. For example, Black and Atkin (1996: 188), in their exploration of curriculum innovation in a number of countries,

> could see how some changes seem to require teachers to change how they operate and their view of themselves as expert professionals. Thus the evidence showed innovations as powerful opportunities – for professional growth or for disorientation, and sometimes for both together. It showed also that teachers can transform innovations as they turn them into manageable classroom practice.

In our case studies of teacher adaptation, curricular conditions were not overtly supportive of teaching socio-scientific issues. However, even when curriculum circumstances are favourable, teachers need support in recognizing the changes in pedagogic style needed and in implementing active learning strategies. In the innovative Science for Public Understanding (SPU) course for post-16 students (AQA 1999) there is overt curriculum support for addressing learning goals related to socio-scientific issues (Chapter 3). Yet evaluation of the first two years of implementation of SPU suggests that science teachers found it difficult to shift their teaching style – from that of conveying, developing and reinforcing accepted scientific knowledge to allowing students to voice and evaluate their value judgements and their understanding of the nature of scientific endeavour (Osborne *et al.* 2002).

The SPU evaluation suggests guidance and support for teachers are needed in:

- developing, constructing and communicating effective arguments and evaluating them;
- supporting students' skills of reading, writing and constructing effective arguments;
- exploring the use and nature of small-group discussion;
- identification of the salient features in media reports of science for their critical evaluation.

We hope that the strategies discussed in this volume have gone some way to addressing this need.

A consistent message emerges from the research evidence – effective teaching about socio-scientific issues involves a knowledgeable, evaluative and supportive attitude on behalf of the teacher and a willingness and ability to engage students in active learning strategies. These attributes need support and development. Provision of suitable learning strategies and student resources is a useful starting point. We suggest that, in considering teaching for science and citizenship, teachers reflect on the following questions:

- Are you able to reflect on your beliefs about teaching and about teaching socio-scientific issues in particular? (See Chapter 6)
- Are the chosen learning goals appropriate to considering socio-scientific issues? (See Chapter 3)
- Are these learning goals recognized and understood by the students and reinforced during the activity? (See Chapters 5 and 6)
- Are you providing students with opportunities to air their views and listen carefully to others? (See Chapters 4 to 7)
- Are you seeking reasoned arguments, allowing students to evaluate arguments of others? (See Chapters 4 to 7)

- Importantly, are you encouraging students to reflect on the outcomes of the activity? (See Chapter 7)
- Are you taking a common-sense approach to eliminate or evaluate bias? (See Chapter 7)
- Can you learn from working with others, sharing teaching strategies, focusing on different perspectives? (See Chapter 8)
- Are you able to give ownership to students and address their concerns in relation to socio-scientific issues?

In the research reported in the case studies, the choice of contexts and tasks was in the hands of the teachers. While this may, inevitably, always be the case, full engagement with socio-scientific issues will only become meaningful when students see the issue as relevant and important to themselves. Giving the students a choice of topics, reacting to their concerns (Chapter 8) and getting them to set the problem are all ways of enhancing student engagement. Familiarity and confidence with structured learning strategies suitable for dealing with socio-scientific issues (as described in Chapter 4) enables the teacher to take students' interests and questions and allow reasoned discussion to ensue.

The students in the cases studies were mainly adolescents. Although there is little research evidence showing how students progress with age in their evaluation of scientific evidence and decision-making about socio-scientific issues, we do consider that discussion of such issues should start at an early age. Addressing socio-scientific issues sporadically in the 14–16 age range is, by itself, insufficient experience. As the outcomes of the case studies show, the particular interventions had limited impact. Rather, steady reinforcement and use of evidence evaluation, ethical reasoning and decision-making skills is more likely to allow students to show progress and recognize the nature and importance of socio-scientific issues.

Is effective teaching achievable?

Actions on behalf of the teacher to address effective teaching of socio-scientific issues may be encouraged or discouraged by local circumstances and political factors. As we have indicated, assessment and curriculum structures impact significantly on teachers' classroom priorities and their ability and willingness to change pedagogical practice.

We return to particular tensions throughout this book – where in the curriculum should socio-scientific issues be located and how can the curriculum support for such teaching be provided? As we have shown, discussion of socio-scientific issues straddles different parts of the formal curriculum. A large-scale survey of headteachers, science teachers, humanities teachers and

PSHE coordinators found that *curricular* barriers relate to the nature of syllabuses, resources and opportunities or constraints to cross-curricular coordination (Levinson and Turner 2001: 26). The consequence is that effective teaching and learning is marginalized. There are a number of ways to overcome this unsatisfactory situation. We could:

- locate socio-scientific issues firmly in one current curriculum subject and provide knowledge and pedagogical support for teachers of that subject;
- locate different aspects of socio-scientific issues in different curriculum subjects (as currently) but develop and support collaboration between these subjects and teachers;
- identify socio-scientific issues as a distinct and new curriculum area.

There are disadvantageous consequences to any of these solutions. In terms of current pedagogical skill, humanities teachers are perhaps those with the greatest pedagogical expertise of the most appropriate learning strategies. Humanities teachers may also be familiar with the citizenship concepts inherent in consideration of socio-scientific issues. However, we consider that understanding of the nature of scientific endeavour is crucial and does need to be developed alongside the study of science concepts – that is, within the science curriculum.

Formal cross-curricular collaboration is the key to the second solution. Teachers in Levinson and Turner's study (2001: 60) suggested two realistic methods of collaboration: coordination by a dedicated team of specialists; and different disciplines dealing with a particular issue over a given time period. Levinson and Turner suggest that formal collaboration may be effective if the following features are in place:

- learning group off formal curriculum timetable;
- planning between teachers of different subject areas, particularly English, RE and science;
- an integrated model of teaching;
- assessment through one particular subject area; and
- equal participation by all teaching partners in terms of decision-making.
  (Levinson and Turner, 2001: 62)

The introduction of the citizenship curriculum in England has required curriculum audits, perhaps a first step to developing cross-curricular approaches. We are currently exploring the opportunities and barriers in collapsing the timetable for a day to allow students to consider the social and ethical aspects of biomedical science supported by science and humanities teachers. The outcomes of this project will give clearer understanding of the pedagogical issues in a combined approach to addressing socio-scientific issues. We consider there is much to be gained from a collaborative and systematic approach to teaching socio-scientific issues.

The third option is both unlikely and difficult to implement. We could postulate socio-scientific issues as a new subject in the guise of citizenship. However, socio-scientific issues are only one part of the citizenship curriculum and are not referenced as such.

The integration of science with values has been shown as what happens in practice when we and our students consider socio-scientific issues (see, for example, Chapter 8). Thus we consider that this integration must take place in effective teaching and learning. On balance, we advocate socio-scientific issues as having a clear and important place within the science curriculum. Science teachers should feel empowered and supported in dealing with controversial issues based in contemporary science.

Implementation of the citizenship curriculum and modification to the science curriculum seem the best hopes for 'science education for citizenship' in the short term. Hollins (2001) outlines national curriculum development to bring contemporary science issues into the science curriculum, some of which has stemmed from consideration of *Beyond 2000* (Millar and Osborne 1998) (see Chapter 2, page 28). Of particular importance is the pilot development of a new GCSE in which 'ideas about science' is a major feature. The core modules of the course are designed 'to prepare students to be "consumers" rather than "producers" of scientific knowledge, with a better sense of the cultural importance of science in shaping our everyday lives and our understanding of ourselves and the universe we inhabit' (Hollins 2001: 22). We consider that the development of this course provides a favourable way forward for science education for citizenship in England and Wales.

Whatever curricular structures are in place, the development of pedagogical expertise in addressing socio-scientific issues is important. Thus, initial teacher education is a very important forum for introducing beginning science teachers to the issues outlined in this book. However, trainee teachers come to initial teacher education with an experience of being a student within a system focused on knowledge and skill acquisition related to science concepts. They may have similar expectations to their students of a typical science lesson – that is dominated by explanatory and investigative practical work and learning large amounts of 'scientific facts'. Few have explored the nature of science in their formal education. We would encourage the refocusing of initial teacher education to address the pedagogical expertise and attitude needed to be towards the right in the dimensions shown in Figure 9.1.

The location of socio-scientific issues in the curriculum has a direct influence on the nature of formal assessment of students' achievements – perhaps the most important factor affecting planning, frequency and nature of instruction. Assessment practice does not always support the given curricular aims, particularly in areas where judgements and reasoned arguments are expected. As Levinson and Turner (2001: 11) found, 'there do not appear to be effective criteria in science syllabuses for assessing the skills and knowledge required to address the social and ethical aspects arising from developments in biomedical research.' This is despite a clear curricular expectation that students will explore such aspects.

Here we could take a pessimistic or optimistic view depending on future actions. A pessimist might argue that the current emphasis on evaluating the output of formal education by the easily measurable in summative national tests will continue to dominate. Even if changes to the curriculum are made to reflect the attributes valued in addressing socio-scientific issues, it requires an assessment system with a new emphasis, one in which few examiners currently have expertise. An optimist would see the introduction of citizenship coursework and proposed changes in emphasis in some science assessment as hope for evolutionary change.

Coping with change has been a constant feature of education for many years. As teachers, we can end up being torn between two perspectives – dissatisfied with current curriculum and assessment arrangements and yearning for change which reflects students' interests and future needs; stressed and disorientated through managing yet another curriculum initiative which requires additional work. We find ourselves in a similar situation in making recommendations. We know that wholesale change is unlikely and impractical without willing converts and substantial support. What we have offered throughout this volume are strategies to support evolutionary change – the best we can hope for. Evolutionary change allows evaluation of change at small and large scale. But it does run the risk of not keeping in step with scientific and societal advancements.

One particular rapidly changing area, which has had scant mention in this book, is that of Information and Communication Technology (ICT). It is notable that none of the case studies of practice used ICT resources or pedagogy. One reason was the state of ICT facilities and the low frequency of teacher use of ICT in general at the time of the study. However, this situation is rapidly changing both in schools and for students in their activities outside school.

The issues of dealing with incomplete and biased media information discussed earlier (Chapters 1, 4 and 7) do not change when dealing with the information overload possible from Internet searching, and email communication with people with a wide variety of expertise and viewpoints. However, abilities to search effectively and evaluate fully become more crucial when faced with potentially overwhelming sources of information. Although we have not dealt with use of ICT as a learning strategy in its own right, we consider the principles we have discussed in evaluating media reports apply. In essence, the learning goals we have discussed become more important if future citizens have increased access to a huge variety of information sources.

We cannot predict what socio-scientific issues may be on the agenda for public discussion in five or ten years' time. What we do think will remain important is development of critical evaluation skills based on integration of relevant understanding of the nature of science, citizenship and sustainability with consideration of attitudes and beliefs.

References

Addinell, S. and Solomon, J. (eds) (1983) *Science in a Social Context. Teacher's Guide.* Hatfield: Association for Science Education.

Advisory Group on Citizenship (1998) *Education for Citizenship and the Teaching of Democracy in Schools*, Final Report. London: The Stationery Office.

Aikenhead, G.S. (1991) *Logical Reasoning in Science and Technology (LoRST)*. Toronto: John Wiley.

Aikenhead, G.S. (1994) Critical thinking, decision-making and constructivism in a new STS science course, in *Papers Submitted to the 6th IOSTE Symposium on World Trends in Science and Technology Education* at Palm Springs, CA, 1991. Enschede, Netherlands: National Institute for Curriculum Development.

AQA (Assessment and Qualifications Alliance) (1999) *Specification for GCE Science for Public Understanding*. Manchester: AQA.

AQA (Assessment and Qualifications Alliance) (2001) *Specification for GCSE Citizenship* Assessment and Qualifications Alliance. Manchester: AQA.

ASE (Association for Science Education) (2002) *Can We; Should We? CD ROM for Science Year – No. 3*. Hatfield: ASE.

Baron, J. and Brown, R.V. (1991) *Teaching Decision-making to Adolescents*. Hillsdale, NJ: Lawrence Erlbaum Associates.

Bartholomew, H., Osborne, J. and Ratcliffe, M. (2002) Teaching pupils 'ideas-about-science': case studies from the classroom. Paper presented at the Annual Conference of the National Association for Research in Science Teaching, New Orleans, April 7–10.

Beyth-Marom, R., Fischoff, B., Jacobs Quadrel, M. and Furby, L. (1991) Teaching decision-making to adolescents: a critical review, in J. Baron and R. Brown *Teaching Decision-making to Adolescents*. Hillsdale, NJ: Lawrence Erlbaum Associates.

Biggs, J.B. and Collis, K.F. (1982) *Evaluating the Quality of Learning*. London: Academic Press.

Black, P. and Atkin, J.M. (eds) (1996) *Changing the Subject. Innovations in Science, Mathematics and Technology Education*. London: Routledge.

Black, P. and Wiliam, D. (1998) *Inside the Black Box – Raising Standards Through Classroom Assessment*. London: King's College.

Blythman, J. (2001) Toxic shock, *Guardian*, 20 October.

BMA (British Medical Association) (1990) *The BMA Guide to Living with Risk*. London: Penguin

Bonnett, M. and Williams, J. (1998) Environmental education and primary children's attitudes towards nature and the environment, *Cambridge Journal of Education*, 28(2): 159–74.

Bridges, D. (1979) *Education, Democracy and Discussion*. Windsor: NFER Publishing Company.

Brignell, J. (2000) *Sorry, Wrong Number! The Abuse of Measurement*. Great Britain: Brignell Associates in cooperation with the European Science and Environment Forum.

Brody, M.J. (1994) Student science knowledge related to ecological crises, *International Journal of Science Education*, 16(4): 421–35.

Cade, A. (1990) Listening to children – the young opinion formers on Earth, *Annual Review of Environmental Education*, 3: 10–11, Reading: Council for Environmental Education.

Callicott, J.B. (1997) Conservation values and ethics, in G.K. Meffe and C.R. Carroll (eds) *Principles of Conservation Biology*. Sunderland, MA: Sinauer.

Chawla, L. (1999) Life paths into effective environmental action, *Journal of Environmental Education*, 31 (1): 15–26.

Cooper, G. (1994) The role of outdoor education in education for the 21st century, *Environmental Education*, 46 (Summer): 28–31.

Cornell, J. (1989) *Sharing the Joy of Nature: Nature Activities for all Ages*. Nevada City, CA: Dawn Publications.

Crick, B. (2000) *Essays on Citizenship*. London: Continuum.

Crick, B. (2001) Citizenship and science; science and citizenship, *School Science Review*, 83(302): 33–8.

Cross, R.T. and Price, R.F. (1999) The social responsibility of science and the public understanding of science, *International Journal of Science Education*, 21(7): 775–85.

Dawson, C. (2000) Selling snake oil: must science educators continue to promise what they can't deliver?, *Melbourne Studies in Education*, 41(2): 121–32, Special Issue: Science and the Citizen.

DETR (Department of the Environment, Transport and the Regions) (1999) *Sustainable Development Education Panel: First Annual Report 1998*. Norwich: The Stationery Office.

DfEE/QCA (Department for Education and Employment/Qualifications and Curriculum Authority) (1999) *The National Curriculum for England: Citizenship*. London: The Stationery Office.

Driver, R., Leach, J., Millar, R., and Scott, P. (1996) *Young People's Images of Science*. Buckingham: Open University Press.

Driver, R., Squires, A., Rushworth, P. and Wood-Robinson, V. (1994) *Making Sense of Secondary Science*. London: Routledge.

Durant, J.R., Evans, G.A. and Thomas, G.P. (1989) The public understanding of science, *Nature*, 340, 6 July: 11–14.

Durant, J. (1996) 'Red faces, white coats and blue funk', *Times Higher Education Review*, 5 April: 14–15.

Durant, J. and Lindsey, N. (2000) *The 'Great GM Food Debate': a survey of media coverage in the first half of 1999, POST Report 138*. London: Parliamentary Office of Science and Technology.

Eagles, P.F.J. and Demare, R. (1999) Factors influencing children's environmental attitudes, *Journal of Environmental Education*, 30(4): 33–7.

Edexcel (2001) *Specification for GCSE Citizenship*. London: Edexcel Foundation.

Fien, J. (1993a) *Environmental Education: A Pathway to Sustainability?* Geelong, Australia: Deakin University Press.

Fien, J. (1993b) *Education for the Environment, Critical Curriculum Theorizing and Environmental Education*. Geelong, Australia: Deakin University Press.

Findlay, J.J. (1920) *An Introduction to Sociology for Social Workers and General Readers*. Manchester: Manchester University Press.

Fleming, R. (1986) Adolescent reasoning in socio-scientific issues, Part I: Social cognition, *Journal of Research in Science Teaching*, 23(8): 677–87.

Food Link News (2000) *Food Link News* 32 (Newsletter for the Food Link programme), MAFF publications from www.defra.gov.uk (accessed 4 June 2002).

Freeman, C. (1995) The changing nature of children's environmental experience: the shrinking realm of outdoor play, *Environmental Education and Information*, 14 (3): 259–80.

Fullick, P.L. and Ratcliffe, M. (eds) (1996) *Teaching Ethical Aspects of Science*. Totton: Bassett Press.

Gayford, C.G. (1991) Environmental education: a question of emphasis in the school curriculum, *Cambridge Journal of Education*, 21: 73–9.

Grace, M. and Ratcliffe, M. (2002) The science and values that young people draw upon to make decisions about biological conservation issues, *International Journal of Science Education*, 24(11): 1157–69.

Grace, M. and Sharp, J. (2000a) Exploring the actual and potential rhetoric–reality gaps in environmental education and their implications for pre-service teacher training, *Environmental Education Research*, 6(4): 331–45.

Grace, M. and Sharp, J. (2000b) Young people's views on the importance of conserving biodiversity, *School Science Review*, 82(298): 49–56.

Greaves, E., Stanisstreet, M., Boyes, E. and Williams, T.R. (1993) Children's ideas about animal conservation, *School Science Review*, 75(271): 51–60.

Harrison, C. (1993) Nature conservation, science and popular values in F.B. Goldsmith and A. Warren (eds) *Conservation in Progress*. Chichester: Wiley.

Heater, D. (1999) *What is Citizenship?* Cambridge: Polity Press.

Hirokawa, R.Y. and Scheerhorn D.R. (1986) Communication in faulty group decision-making, in R. Hirokawa and M. Poole (eds) *Communication and Group Decision-making*. Beverly Hills: Sage Publications.

Hollins, M. (2001) School science in step with the changing world of the 21st century. A curriculum development project by QCA *Education in Science*, 194: 22–3.

Huckle, J. (1985) Geography and schooling, in R. Johnston (ed.) *The Future of Geography*. London: Methuen.

Huckle, J. (2001) Towards ecological citizenship, in D. Lambert and P. Machon (eds) *Citizenship through Secondary Geography*. London: Routledge/Falmer.

Huckle, J. and Sterling, S. (eds) (1997) *Education for Sustainability*. London: Earthscan.

Hunt, A. and Millar, R. (eds) (2000) *AS Science for Public Understanding*. London: Heinemann.

Irwin, A. and Wynne, B. (eds) (1996) *Misunderstanding Science?* Cambridge: Cambridge University Press.

IUCN (International Union for Conservation of Nature and Natural Resources) (1980) *World Conservation Strategy: Living resource conservation for sustainable development*. Gland, Switzerland: IUCN.

IUCN (International Union for Conservation of Nature and Natural Resources)/ UNEP (United Nations Environment Programme)/WWF (Worldwide Fund for Nature) (1991) *Caring for the Earth: A Strategy for Sustainable Living*. Gland, Switzerland: Earthscan.

Janis, I.L. (1968) Attitude change via role-playing, in R.P Abelson (ed.) *Theories of Cognitive Consistency: A Sourcebook*. Chicago, IL: Rand McNally.

Jenkins, E. (1997) Scientific and technological literacy for citizenship: what can we learn from research and other evidence?, in S. Sjoberg and E. Kallerud (eds) *Science, Technology and Citizenship*. Oslo: Norwegian Institute for Studies in Research and Higher Education.

Joyce, B. and Showers, B. (1995) *Student Achievement through Staff Development* (2nd ed). White Plains, NY: Longman.

Kerr, D. (1999) *Re-examining Citizenship Education: The Case of England*. Slough: National Foundation for Educational Research.

Koker, M. (1996) Students' decisions about environmental issues and problems – an evaluation study of the Science Education for Public Understanding (SEPUP) Programme. Unpublished PhD thesis, University of Southampton.

Kolstoe, S.D. (2000) Consensus projects: teaching science for citizenship, *International Journal of Science Education*, 22(6): 645–64.

Korpan, C.A., Bisanz, G.L., Bisanz, J. and Henderson, J.M. (1997) Assessing literacy in science: evaluation of scientific news briefs, *Science Education*, 81: 515–32.

Kuhn, D., Amsel, E. and O'Loghlin, M. (1988) *The Development of Scientific Thinking Skills*. London: Academic Press.

Lantz, O. and Kass, H. (1987) Chemistry teachers' functional paradigms, *Science Education*, 71(1): 117–34.

Laugksch, R. (2000) Scientific literacy: a conceptual overview, *Science and Education*, 84: 71–94.

Law, N., Fensham, P., Li, S. and Wei, B. (2000) Public understanding of science as basic literacy, *Melbourne Studies in Education*, 41(2): 145–55, Special Issue: Science and the Citizen.

Lawson, H. (2001) Active citizenship in schools and the community, *The Curriculum Journal*, 12(2): 163–78.

Layton, D. (1986) Revaluing science education, in P. Tomlinson and M. Quinton (eds) *Values Across the Curriculum*. London: Falmer Press.

Layton, D. (1994) STS in the school curriculum: a movement overtaken by history?, in J. Solomon and G. Aikenhead (eds) *STS Education International Perspectives on Reform*. New York: Teachers College Press.

Layton, D., Jenkins, E., Macgill, S. and Davey, A. (1993) *Inarticulate Science? Perspectives on the Public Understanding of Science and Some Implications for School Science*. Driffield: Driffield Press.

Leat, D. (ed.) (2000) *Thinking through Geography*. Cambridge: Chris Kington Publishing.

Levinson, R. and Thomas, J. (eds) (1997) *Science Today*. London: Routledge.

Levinson, R. and Turner, S. (2001) *Valuable Lessons: Engaging with the Social Context of Science in Schools*. London: The Wellcome Trust.

Lumpe, A.T., Haney, J.J. and Czerniak, C.M. (1998) Science teacher beliefs and intentions to implement Science–Technology–Society (STS) in the classroom, *Journal of Science Teacher Education*, 9(1): 1–24.

Lynch, J. (1992) *Education for Citizenship in a Multi-cultural Society*. London: Cassell.

McClune, B. and Jarman, R. (2001) Making a place for newspapers in secondary science education, in O. de Jong, E.R. Savelsbergh and A. Alblas (eds) *Teaching for Scientific Literacy*. Utrecht: CD-β Press.

McComas, W. (1998) The principal elements of the nature of science: dispelling the myths, in W. McComas (ed.) *The Nature of Science in Science Education: Rationales and Strategies*. Dordrecht: Kluwer Academic Press.

McComas, W., Clough, M.P. and Almazroa, H. (1998) The role and character of the nature of science in science education in W. McComas, *The Nature of Science in Science Education: Rationales and Strategies*. Dordrecht: Kluwer Academic Press.

McGivney, V. (1993) Participation and non-participation: a review of the literature, in R. Edwards, S. Sieminski and D. Zeldin, *Adult Learners, Education and Training*. Buckingham: Open University Press.

Mann, L., Harmoni, R., Power, C., Beswick, G. and Ormond, C. (1988) Effectiveness of the GOFER course in decision-making for high school students, *Journal of Behavioral Decision Making*, 1: 159–68.

Marsden, B. (2001) Citizenship education: historical pointers, in D. Lambert and P. Machon (eds) *Citizenship through Secondary Geography*. London: Routledge/Falmer.

Millar, R. and Osborne, J.F. (eds) (1998) *Beyond 2000: Science Education for the Future*. London: King's College.

Morris, M. and Schagen, I. (1996) *Green Attitudes or Learned Responses? Global Environmental Education*. Berkshire: National Foundation for Education Research.

Neal, P. and Palmer, J. (1990) *Environmental Education in the Primary School*. Oxford: Blackwell Education.

Nelkin, D. (1995) *Selling Science. How the Press Covers Science and Technology*. New York: W.H. Freeman and Company.

Norris, S.P. and Phillips, L.M. (1994) Interpreting pragmatic meaning when reading popular reports of science, *Journal of Research in Science Teaching*, 31(9): 947–67.

Nott, M. and Wellington, J. (1997) Critical incidents in the science classroom and the nature of science, *School Science Review* 76 (276): 41–6.

OCR (Oxford, Cambridge and RSA Examinations) (2000a) *History A (Schools History Project) Specimen Paper 2 and Mark Scheme 2003*. Cambridge: OCR.

OCR (Oxford, Cambridge and RSA Examinations) (2000b) *Science Double Award, Salters Higher Tier Specimen Paper and Mark Scheme 2003*. Cambridge: OCR.

OCR (Oxford, Cambridge and RSA Examinations) (2001) *Geography A, Foundation Tier Specimen Paper and Mark Scheme 2003*. Cambridge: OCR.

Ofsted (Office for Standards in Education) (2002a) *Standards and Quality in Education 2000/1: The Annual Report of Her Majesty's Chief Inspector of Schools*. Norwich: The Stationery Office.

Ofsted (2002b) *Changing Schools: An evaluation of the Effectiveness of Transfer Arrangements at Age 11*. Norwich: The Stationery Office.

Osborne, J., Duschl, R. and Fairbrother, B. (2002) *Breaking the Mould? Teaching Science for Public Understanding*. London: King's College.

Osborne, J. and Ratcliffe, M. (2002) Developing effective methods of assessing ideas and evidence, *School Science Review*, 83(305): 113–23.

Osborne, J., Ratcliffe, M., Collins, S., Millar, R. and Duschl, R. (2001) *What Should We Teach about Science? A Delphi Study*. www.york.ac.uk/depts/educ/projs/EPSE (accessed 20 September 2002).

Osler, A. (2000) *Citizenship and Democracy in Schools: Diversity, Identity, Equality*. Stoke-on-Trent: Trentham Books.

OST (Office of Science and Technology)/The Wellcome Trust (2000) *Science and the Public: A Review of Science Communication and Public Attitudes to Science*. London: The Wellcome Trust.

Oulton, C. R. and Scott, W.A.H. (1994) Improving teachers' contribution to environmental education, *Teacher Development*, 3(1): 23–9.

Oxfam (1997) *A Curriculum for Global Citizenship*. London: Oxfam.

Palmer, J.A. (1998) *Environmental Education in the 21st Century. Theory, Practice, Progress and Promise*. London: Routledge.

Palmer, J.A. and Neal, P. (1994) *The Handbook of Environmental Education*. London: Routledge.

Phillips, L.M. and Norris, S.P. (1999) Interpreting popular reports of science: what happens when the reader's world meets the world on paper, *International Journal of Science Education*, 21(3): 317–27.

Philo, G. (ed.) (1998) *Message Received*. Harlow: Longman.

PISA (Programme for International Student Assessment) (2002) www.pisa.oecd.org (accessed 20 September 2002).

PRI (Pupil Researcher Initiative) (2001) *Ideas and Evidence Science Pack, CDROM.* London: Collins Educational.

QCA (Qualifications and Curriculum Authority) (2000) *Citizenship at Key Stages 3 and 4: Initial Guidance for Schools.* London: QCA.

QCA (Qualifications and Curriculum Authority) (2002) http://www.standards.dfee.gov.uk/schemes/ (accessed 3 September 2002).

Ratcliffe, M. (1996) Adolescent decision-making, by individuals and groups, about science-related social issues, in G. Welford, J. Osborne and P. Scott (eds) *Research in Science Education in Europe.* London: Falmer Press.

Ratcliffe, M. (1997) Pupil decision-making about socio-scientific issues within the science curriculum, *International Journal of Science Education,* 19(2): 167–82.

Ratcliffe, M. (1999) Evaluation of abilities in interpreting media reports of scientific research, *International Journal of Science Education,* 21(10): 1085–99.

Ratcliffe, M. (2001) Science, technology and society in school science education, *School Science Review,* 82(300): 83–92.

Ratcliffe, M. (2002) Teaching for understanding in scientific enquiry, in S. Amos and R. Boohan (eds) *Aspects of Teaching Secondary Science: Perspectives on Practice.* London: Routledge/Falmer.

Robertson, C.L. and Krugly-Smolska, E. (1997) Gaps between advocated practices and teaching realities in environmental education, *Environmental Education Research,* 3(3): 311–26.

Royal Society (1992) *Risk: Analysis, Perception and Management.* London: Royal Society.

Rudduck, J. (1986) A strategy for handling controversial issues in the secondary school, in J. Wellington (ed.) *Controversial Issues in the Curriculum.* Oxford: Basil Blackwell.

Sadler, R. (1989) Formative assessment and the design of instructional systems, *Instructional Science,* 18: 119–44.

Samarapungavan, A. (1992) Children's judgement in theory choice tasks: scientific rationality in childhood, *Cognition,* 45: 1–32.

Savelsbergh, E., de Jong, O., Albas, A. (2001) Teaching for scientific literacy: an introduction, in O. de Jong, E.R. Savelsbergh and A. Alblas (eds) *Teaching for Scientific Literacy,* Utrecht: CD-β Press.

Science in Society (1981) *Teacher's Guide.* London: Heinemann/Association for Science Education.

Shamos, M.H. (1995) *The Myth of Scientific Literacy.* New Brunswick: Rutgers University Press.

Simmons, D. (1994) Urban children's preferences for nature: lessons for environmental education, *Children's Environments,* 11(3): 194–203.

Simpson, S. (1985) Short-term wilderness experiences and environmental ethics, *Journal of Experiential Education,* 8(3): 25–8.

Solomon, J. (1992a) *Getting to Know about Energy*. London: Falmer Press.

Solomon, J. (1992b) The classroom discussion of science-based social issues presented on television: knowledge, attitudes and values, *International Journal of Science Education*, 14(4): 431–44.

Solomon, J. (1992c) *How Does Society Decide?* Hatfield: Association for Science Education.

Solomon, J. (1993) *Teaching Science, Technology and Society*. Buckingham: Open University Press.

Solomon, J. (1994) Towards a map of problems in STS research, in J. Solomon and G. Aikenhead (eds) *STS Education International Perspectives on Reform*. New York: Teachers College Press.

Solomon, J. and Aikenhead, G. (eds) (1994) *STS Education International Perspectives on Reform*. New York: Teachers College Press.

Solomon, J., Scott, L. and Duveen, J. (1996) Large-scale exploration of pupils' understanding of the nature of science, *Science Education*, 80(5): 493–508.

Spellerberg, I.F. (1996) *Conservation Biology*. Harlow: Longman.

Stanisstreet, M., Spofforth, N. and Williams, T. (1993) Attitudes of children to the uses of animals, *International Journal of Science Education*, 15(4): 411–25.

Stenhouse, L. (1970) *The Humanities Curriculum Project: An Introduction*. London: Heinemann.

Sterling, S. (1996) Education in change, in J. Huckle and S. Sterling (eds) *Education for Sustainability*. London: Earthscan Publications Limited.

Swets, J.A. (1991) Normative decision-making, in J. Baron and R. Brown (eds) *Teaching Decision-making to Adolescents*. Hillsdale, NJ: Lawrence Erlbaum Associates.

Symons, G. (1997) *Sustainability in Action in Britain?* Godalming: WWF-UK.

Thorp, S. (ed.) (1991) *Race, Equality and Science Teaching*. Hatfield: Association for Science Education.

Tilbury, D. (1995) Environmental education for sustainability: defining the new focus of environmental education in the 1990s, *Environmental Education Research*, 1(2): 195–212.

Tomlins, B. and Froud, K. (1994) *Environmental Education: Teaching Approaches and Students' Attitudes*. Slough: National Foundation for Educational Research.

UNEP (United Nations Environment Programme) (1995) *Global Biodiversity Assessment*. Cambridge: Cambridge University Press.

Van Matre, S. (1990) *Earth Education: A New Beginning*. USA: Institute for Earth Education.

Warnock, M. (2001) *An Intelligent Person's Guide to Ethics*. London: Duckbacks.

WCED (World Commission on Environment and Development) (1987) *Our Common Future*. Oxford: Oxford University Press.

Wellington, J.J. (ed.) (1986) *Controversial Issues in the Curriculum*. London: Blackwell.

Wellington, J. and Osborne, J. (2001) *Language and Literacy in Science Education.* Buckingham: Open University Press.

Wilson, M. and Draney, K. (1997). Developing maps for student progress in the SEPUP assessment system. Paper presented to the annual meeting of the American Association for the Advancement of Science, Seattle, WA.

Yearly, S. (1991) *The Green Case.* London: HarperCollins Academic.

Index

LANGUAGE AND LITERACY IN SCIENCE EDUCATION

Jerry Wellington and Jonathan Osborne

All teachers look and hope for more scientific forms of expression and reasoning from their pupils, but few have been taught specific techniques for supporting students' use of scientific language. This book is full of them . . . In this very practical book, Jerry Wellington and Jonathan Osborne do much more than summarize research which shows how very much language, in all its forms, matters to science education. They also show teachers what can be done to make learning science through language both more effective and more enjoyable.

> Jay L. Lemke, Professor of Education, City University of New York

Science in secondary schools has tended to be viewed mainly as a 'practical subject', and language and literacy in science education have been neglected. But learning the language of science is a major part of science education: every science lesson is a language lesson, and language is a major barrier to most school students in learning science. This accessible book explores the main difficulties in the language of science and examines practical ways to aid students in retaining, understanding, reading, speaking and writing scientific language.

Jerry Wellington and Jonathan Osborne draw together and synthesize current good practice, thinking and research in this field. They use many practical examples, illustrations and tried-and-tested materials to exemplify principles and to provide guidelines in developing language and literacy in the learning of science. They also consider the impact that the growing use of information and communications technology has had, and will have, on writing, reading and information handling in science lessons.

The authors argue that paying more attention to language in science classrooms is one of the most important acts in improving the quality of science education. This is a significant and very readable book for all student and practising secondary school science teachers, for science advisers and school mentors.

Contents

Acknowledgements – Introduction: the importance of language in science education – Looking at the language of science – Talk of the classroom: language interactions between teachers and pupils – Learning from reading – Writing for learning in science – Discussion in school science: learning science through talking – Writing text for learning science – Practical ploys for the classroom – Last thoughts . . . – References – Appendix – Index.

160pp   0 335 20598 4 (Paperback)   0 335 20599 2 (Hardback)

YOUNG PEOPLE'S IMAGES OF SCIENCE

Rosalind Driver, John Leach, Robin Millar and Phil Scott

- What ideas about science do school students form as a result of their experiences in and out of school?
- How might science teaching in schools develop a more scientifically-literate society?
- How do school students understand disputes about scientific issues including those which have social significance, such as the irradiation of food?

There have been calls in the UK and elsewhere for a greater public understanding of science underpinned by, amongst other things, school science education. However, the relationship between school science, scientific literacy and the public understanding of science remains controversial.

In this book, the authors argue that an understanding of science goes beyond learning the facts, laws and theories of science and that it involves understanding the nature of scientific knowledge itself and the relationships between science and society. Results of a major study into the understanding of these issues by school students aged 9 to 16 are described. These results suggest that the success of the school science curriculum in promoting this kind of understanding is at best limited.

The book concludes by discussing ways in which the school science curriculum could be adapted to better equip students as future citizens in our modern scientific and technological society. It will be particularly relevant to science teachers, advisers and inspectors, teacher educators and curriculum planners.

Contents
Introduction – Why does understanding the nature of science matter? – Perspectives on the nature of science – What do we already know about students' understanding of the nature of science – Investigating students' ideas about the nature of science – Students' characterizations of the purposes of scientific work – Students' views of the nature and status of scientific knowledge – A framework for characterizing features of students' epistemological reasoning in science – Students' views of science as a social enterprise – Young people's images of the nature of science: implications for science education – References – Appendix – Index.

192pp   0 335 19381 1 (Paperback)   0 335 19382 X (Hardback)

GOOD PRACTICE IN SCIENCE TEACHING
WHAT RESEARCH HAS TO SAY

Martin Monk and Jonathan Osborne (eds)

This book offers a summary of major educational research and scholarship important to the field of science education. Written, in a clear, concise and readable style, the authors have identified the principal messages and their implications for the practice of science teaching. Aimed at science teachers of children of all ages, and others who work in teaching and related fields, the book provides an invaluable first guide for science teachers. All of the chapters are written by authors from King's College and the University of Leeds, both of which are institutions with an international reputation for their work in the field with top research ratings. Each chapter summarises the research work and evidence in the field, discussing its significance, reliability and implications. Valuable lists of further reading and full references are provided at the end of each chapter.

Contents

Introduction – Part one: The science classroom – Strategies for learning – Formative assessment – Children's thinking, learning, teaching and constructivism – The role of practical work – The nature of scientific knowledge – The role of language in the learning and teaching of science – Students' attitudes towards science – Part two: The science department – Managing the science department – Summative assessment – Science teaching and the development of intelligence – Progression and differentiation – Information and communications technologies: their role and value for science educa-tion – Part three: The science world – GNVQ Science at Advanced level: a new kind of course – Science for citizenship – Index.

256pp   0 335 20391 4 (Paperback)   0 335 20392 2 (Hardback)

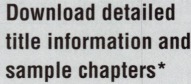